The Military Life of

JULIUS CAESAR,

IMPERATOR

by TREVOR NEVITT DUPUY
Col., U.S. Army, Ret.

BARNES
&NOBLE
BOOKS
NEW YORK

This book is dedicated to
Grace P. Hayes

Maps by Dyno Lowenstein

This edition published by Barnes & Noble, Inc.
by arrangement with Franklin Watts Inc.

1996 Barnes & Noble Books

ISBN 0-76070-058-3

Printed and bound in the United States of America.
M 9 8 7 6 5 4 3 2 1
FG

Contents

Foreword

One of the most fascinating, enigmatic, and controversial figures of history is Caius Julius Caesar. He was also one of the very greatest soldiers in the annals of warfare, and is the third great captain to be included in this series of military biographies.

Although there are some gaps in our knowledge of Caesar's life, its principal events are better documented than those of either Alexander or Hannibal. The most important source is the *Commentaries* of Caesar himself, one of the most important autobiographical works in existence. The *Commentaries* must be read with some caution, of course, because Caesar quite naturally presents a highly subjective view of some very controversial activities. Nevertheless, internal consistency, as well as the supporting evidence of archeology and of other documents, indicates that Caesar is quite accurate and highly reliable in the presentation of facts.

Since he was one of the giants of history, many books have been written about Caesar, and about the stirring events in which he participated. In written history and in romantic literature he has been presented as one of the world's greatest heroes as well as one of its greatest villains. In this work I have tried to avoid an evaluation of his personal character, save as it is related to the military events which earned him a reputation as a great captain.

There have been two important analyses of Caesar's generalship, by two of the most respected military historians of the past century, and both have been valuable sources for this work. The one by Theodore Ayrault Dodge is generally somewhat more favorable to Caesar than that by J.F.C. Fuller. I have also relied heavily on prior research which I have done in connection with the preparation of an *Encyclopedia of Military History,* as coauthor with R. Ernest Dupuy.

Among other sources consulted in the process of current or prior research are the following: Chester Starr's *A History of the Ancient World*; Plutarch's *Life of Julius Caesar*; Frank Frost Abbott's *A History and Description of Roman Political Institutions*; M. Rostovtzeff's *Rome*; Volume IX of the *Cambridge Ancient History*; and M. Cary's *A Shorter History of Rome.*

I am grateful to Grace P. Hayes for her thoughtful comments and great substantive contributions to this work. Another important contribution has been her critical view of Caesar as a person, which has helped prevent me from letting hero worship sway my objective, historical, and military professional judgment of the man and his accomplishments.

T. N. DUPUY

Introduction

Plutarch, the ancient biographer, evaluated Julius Caesar as a general who was "not in the least inferior to any of the greatest and most admired commanders who had ever appeared at the head of armies. For if we compare him," wrote Plutarch, "with the Fabii, the Metelli, the Scipios, and with those who were his contemporaries, nor not long before him, Sulla, Marius, the Luculli, or even Pompey himself, whose glory, it may be said, went up at that time to heaven for every excellence in war, we shall find Caesar's actions to have surpassed them all."

Had Caesar been only a military man, his place in history, as Plutarch indicates, would be secure. But in addition, Caesar's driving ambition secured for him absolute leadership of the most powerful nation in the world.

Historians differ sharply in their evaluations of Caesar. His detractors believe that he was an utterly selfish and unscrupulous man, an opportunist who was motivated by nothing other than lust for power and wealth. They point to the many atrocities committed under his orders, or with his approval, as evidence that Caesar was a cruel man, with little respect for human life or dignity.

Caesar's admirers believe that his was the healthy ambition of a strong but patriotic man, who seized an opportunity to improve the lot of the downtrodden common people of Rome, and sought to bring to an end the turmoil that had shaken Rome to its foundations during the first half of the first century B.C. They see Caesar as a wise and benevolent ruler and an honorable and magnanimous conqueror, less bloodthirsty and more considerate of defeated foes than were most of the great Romans who preceded him and who followed him. As to his strength of character, they believe this was evidenced by the first important act of his adult life—his willingness to risk death and dishonor rather than to give up his wife at the command of an autocratic dictator.

Whatever one may think of Caesar as a politican and as a historical figure, he was clearly one of the most gifted human beings who ever walked the face of the earth. He was a successful lawyer. He was a brilliant orator. He was one of the most influential, popular, and successful politicians in history. He held the leading religious office in Rome. He was a writer whose works are recognized as literary classics, and also as historical documents whose accuracy has been constantly confirmed by archeological discoveries.

Above all, Caesar was one of the greatest and most successful military leaders who ever lived, and it is his military career that concerns us in this book. It was a most unusual one.

Except for very limited military service expected of all young

Roman citizens, Caesar displayed neither interest nor talent in military affairs until he was in his fortieth year. In the following sixteen years he literally taught himself the art of war. It was an art to which he readily adapted himself, due to an exceptionally brilliant intellect and other superior talents.

Partly because of the lateness of his turn to military matters, and partly because of his nature, Caesar was probably not as great a strategist or tactician as the other two great captains of antiquity: Alexander and Hannibal. But he shared all of their other qualities as military leaders. He perhaps even exceeded them and every other general of history in his ability as a leader to inspire soldiers to perform seemingly impossible feats in battle.*

Caesar's one possible serious shortcoming as a military commander was a tendency toward rashness. But this was often merely self-confidence based upon an objective evaluation of his own exceptional abilities. Although this apparent rashness exposed him to many close calls, and sometimes brought him to the brink of disaster, he always emerged successful and triumphant. Certainly he was lucky, probably the luckiest general in history, and luck played a great part in many of these hair-breadth escapes. But it does seem strange that luck would always favor Caesar, and never his opponents.

The fact is, Caesar made his own luck. Convinced of the importance of seizing the initiative whenever possible, he always calculated the odds of success closely, and then improved

* See Appendix for definitions of strategy and tactics, and for a discussion of the qualities of military leadership.

xi

on those odds by vigor, speed, and an ability to make sound, lightning decisions in moments of great stress.

In the following chapters the thoughtful reader will notice how many times Caesar displayed commendable caution in circumstances in which he apparently figured that the odds were not sufficiently favorable for bold action. The reader will also notice how often Caesar used good sound common sense, plus great military skill, to change these circumstances. Then, when "the die was cast," no soldier of antiquity or modern times could excel his boldness, speed, or determination in taking advantage of the circumstances he had created.

THE MILITARY LIFE OF

JULIUS CAESAR,

IMPERATOR

CHAPTER 1

Defiance to Sulla

Priest and Dictator

Early in the year 81 B.C. the self-appointed dictator of Rome, the great general L. Cornelius Sulla, sent for the Priest of Jupiter. At that time this important religious position in the Roman Republic was held by an exceedingly young, but capable young man, Caius Julius Caesar, then barely twenty years old. Caesar had been appointed to his priestly duties about three years earlier because he was a member of a leading Roman family, and because he had been an ardent supporter of the previous Roman dictator, Gaius Marius—who had been Sulla's most bitter foe in a series of prolonged struggles for control of Rome. Two years later Caesar had married the daughter of L. Cornelius Cinna, who, before his death in the civil war, had been a close associate of Marius, and a deadly personal enemy of Sulla.

Because of his close past connection with Sulla's enemies, young Julius Caesar must have wondered what would happen to him as he appeared before the dictator. He certainly knew that Sulla—who could do nothing to punish his now-dead

3

enemies, Marius and Cinna—had been ordering the execution of many of their followers. Caesar must have feared a like fate for himself.

However, Sulla apparently received the young priest cordially. He informed Julius that he could remain the Priest of Jupiter, but that he must divorce his wife, since she was Cinna's daughter.

Caesar was an ambitious young man—but he was also proud, and he loved his wife. We do not know how long he pondered Sulla's order, but he and his wife soon fled Rome. Sulla, enraged, ordered Caesar to be discharged from his priesthood, and seized all of his property. The dictator sent troops to pursue the fugitives and a few days later Caesar was captured and again led before Sulla. The general seems to have admired Caesar's spirit, however. For his family's sake he spared the young man's life, but banished him from Rome.

Background of the Civil War

Rome was originally ruled by kings, but late in the sixth century B.C. it had become a republic, with two chief magistrates, *consuls*, who were elected annually. Until the Second Punic War—against Carthage and Hannibal—the consuls had had charge of the government and also led the armies in the field. When Rome's increasing power and responsibility made it necessary to increase the number of Roman legions, and to maintain armies in widely separated provinces, command had

4

been extended to other officials. These included outgoing consuls, who were known as *proconsuls* when they served abroad, and *praetors*, who were normally charged with running the judicial system and governing the city in the absence of the consuls. Other important public officials in Rome were the eight *quaestors,* or financial officials, four *aediles* who supervised public works, and ten *tribunes.* These tribunes, elected by the common people (plebeians as opposed to patricians), had the function of protecting the interests of the lower classes by vetoing any unfair laws passed by the patrician Senate. They could also initiate legislation in the popularly elected Assembly. Anyone harming a tribune in any way could be put to death without trial.

The Senate was the most powerful and respected governing body of Rome. The senators were the leading citizens of the city, and included those who had held responsible government positions. The powers and functions of the Senate varied during the first century B.C., but it maintained control over financial matters and always wielded great influence because of its membership of experienced men. Most actual lawmaking, however, was done by the popular Assembly, or *Concilium Plebis.* The relative power of Senate and Assembly varied during these troubled years, depending on whether the conservative and patrician *optimates*, or the liberal, plebeian *populares*, held governmental power.

By the time of Caesar's birth, in 100 B.C., Rome controlled much of the area around the Mediterranean Sea, from Spain to Asia Minor. For administrative purposes the empire was divided

5

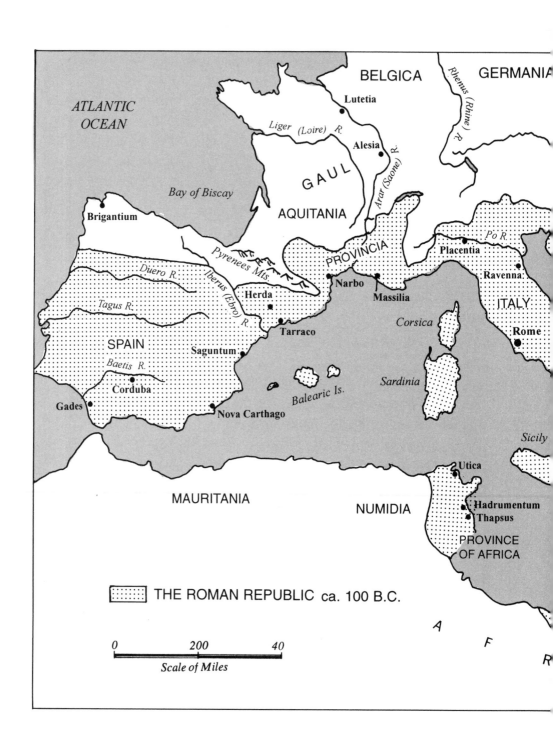

ATLANTIC
OCEAN

BELGICA

GERMANIA

Lutetia

Rhenus (Rhine) R.

Liger (Loire) R.

Alesia

Arar (Saone) R.

G A U L

AQUITANIA

Bay of Biscay

Brigantium

PROVINCIA

Po R.

Placentia

Duero R.

Iberus (Ebro) R.

Pyrenees Mts.

Narbo

Ravenna

Tagus R.

Herda

Massilia

ITALY

Corsica

Rome

Tarraco

SPAIN

Saguntum

Baetis R.

Sardinia

Corduba

Balearic Is.

Gades

Nova Carthago

Sicily

MAURITANIA

NUMIDIA

Utica

Hadrumentum
Thapsus

PROVINCE
OF AFRICA

A

F

R

THE ROMAN REPUBLIC ca. 100 B.C.

0   200   40

Scale of Miles

SARMATIA

DACIA

Danube R.

ILLYRICUM

ADRIATIC SEA

BLACK SEA

THRACE

Dyrrachium

MACEDONIA

Larissa

AEGEAN
SEA

Pharsalus

ASIA MINOR

Myteline

ASIA

Ephesus

CILICIA

Miletus

ACHIA

CARIA

Rhodes

Cyprus

MEDITERRANEAN SEA

Crete

SYRIA

Leptis Minor

Alexandria

CYRENAICA

Nile R.

EGYPT

C   A

in provinces, and a consul or praetor was normally appointed governor of a province after his year in office in Rome. The chief functions of the governor were to keep peace and to raise taxes. Roman tax gatherers were everywhere, and everywhere they were unpopular. Roman merchants had also spread throughout the area, and Rome herself had become a great center of trade. Despite her far-flung interests and responsibilities, however, Rome continued to be governed as a city-state, and the privileges of citizenship were restricted to the residents of Rome herself.

Rome had changed greatly in appearance since 753 B.C., the traditional date of her founding. Many new and costly houses had been built and impressive public buildings were being constructed. No longer was it a small town, for many people from the countryside had moved into the city; foreigners had come there in large numbers; and from all corners of the Mediterranean victorious military leaders had brought back slaves by the thousands. There probably were close to a million inhabitants of Rome in the first century B.C. While wealth had increased and many Romans lived in the greatest luxury, slums had also spread in the city. Domestic servants, factory and shopworkers, and disappointed fortune seekers lived in crowded tenements. Providing the poor with enough to eat was a constant problem of the city government. Money and free entertainment were often offered by city leaders as an easy way to win support of the masses in elections. The lot of most of these poor people was generally miserable. There was a constant danger of mob riots, particularly if free gifts and entertainment were not provided frequently.

A century earlier, during the Second Punic War, a number of the cities of Italy had left Rome to support Hannibal. When these towns were recaptured, much of their territory had been confiscated by Rome, and held as public land. Other areas had been acquired by a few large landholders, often through force, and were being worked by slaves. The sturdy, landowning peasant, source of Rome's armies from the beginning, was disappearing. Toward the end of the second century B.C., two brothers, Tiberius and Gaius Gracchus, had tried unsuccessfully to improve the lot of the poor in Rome by dividing the public lands among them. Both were killed in violent disorders which had become common in Rome.

In 118 B.C., Numidia, a North African kingdom dependent on Rome, rose in rebellion under a prince named Jugurtha. The war dragged on for several years, but in 107 B.C. Gaius Marius was elected consul, and took command in Africa. Up to this time, only citizens who owned property were eligible for service in Roman armies. In order to raise an army sufficiently large to put an end to the war with Jugurtha, Marius abolished the property requirement, and also ended the conscription system that had determined which men would serve. Instead he called for volunteers from the entire population of Rome, laying the groundwork for a professional army. To men from the lowest classes, the army offered a better life than they could expect as civilians. Thus, rather than seeking to serve as short a time as

9

possible, they were anxious to stay as long as possible in military service.

With his new army Marius defeated Jugurtha in a battle in which a brilliant young officer, L. Cornelius Sulla, played an important part. Although guerrilla warfare continued for several years, Jugurtha was finally betrayed to the Romans, and the revolt was suppressed.

In 104 B.C., Marius was again elected consul. He led an army which marched to meet an invasion by the Cimbri and Teutones, two barbarian tribes which had penetrated into northern Italy from Central Europe. After a bitter struggle he defeated the invaders. His victory made him so popular with the common people of Rome that for the next five years he was reelected consul.

Marius was eager to get allotments of public land to reward the veterans of his army but many leading Roman citizens were opposed to this. Nevertheless, he finally succeeded, after making some deals with very questionable politicians. In the elections of 99 B.C., two of the unscrupulous men with whom Marius had been working attempted a coup d'état to overthrow the government. Marius, ordered by the Senate to restore order, arrested his former friends and their supporters, who were subsequently executed. But because of this he lost his other political supporters and went into voluntary exile.

There followed a few years of uneasy peace in Rome, but discord was brewing nearby. The peoples of Italy, who for years had been allies of Rome and who had furnished men to fight for her, had long sought the advantages of Roman citizenship and the Roman laws. In 90 B.C., a number of these Italian cities revolted and set up a separate confederation. The Roman Senate tried to put an end to the revolt by granting citizenship to allies in the states which had not revolted. They then extended these rights to the rebels. But the rebellious tribes and cities were not satisfied, and the three-year Social War followed. The rebellion was finally suppressed in 88 B.C., largely through the military efforts of L. Cornelius Sulla.

Sulla was rewarded in 88 B.C. with a consulship. Then came word that Mithridates VI, king of Pontus in Asia Minor, had stirred up the cities of Greece and Asia Minor into a violent revolt against Rome. Reports reached Rome that some 80,000 Italians—most of them tax gatherers and moneylenders—had been massacred in a single day. To confront this emergency the Roman Senate promptly gave Sulla command of the expedition against Mithridates.

Civil War in Rome

Marius, although almost seventy years old, was jealous of this opportunity to get control of the wealth of Pontus, and was eager to regain his own political prestige in Rome. With some of his supporters he bribed one of the tribunes, P. Sulpicius Rufus, to help him replace Sulla in command of the expedition. As soon as Sulla left Rome to join his army in

11

southern Italy, Sulpicius introduced a law to change the command to Marius. With the support of the liberal group, the populares, the law was passed.

Thanks to Marius' own reforms, however, Sulla now had an army that put loyalty to the general above loyalty to Roman law. When he received orders to surrender his command, Sulla turned his army about and marched to Rome, which he occupied without a fight. Marius fled and Sulpicius was killed. The Assembly obediently repealed the change of command law, and then passed another law prohibiting introduction of any bill in the Assembly without Senate approval. Sulla knew that he could count on the support of the patrician Senators, even when he and his army were away from the city. Then he sailed with his army to Greece.

Hardly had Sulla departed, early in 87 B.C., when the two new consuls, L. Cornelius Cinna and Gnaeus Octavius, quarreled. Cinna was deposed and driven out of Rome. He joined Marius, who had raised an army made up of an unruly band of slaves. Picking up more men from the Italian countryside, the two returned and took over the city. There followed five days of horror. Octavius was murdered and his supporters were slaughtered. Cinna and Marius declared themselves consuls, outlawed Sulla, and repealed his legislation. Marius died soon afterward and many of his followers were put to death by Cinna, who seized complete power.

Sulla, meanwhile, ignored the events in Rome. Driving the forces of Mithridates out of Greece, in 85 B.C. he crossed with his army into Asia Minor and negotiated a peace settlement

12

with the king of Pontus. Then he announced that he was returning to Rome to punish those guilty of crimes against him. Meanwhile Cinna had been killed during a mutiny of soldiers.

Sulla landed at Brundisium in 83 B.C. and found the two new consuls, successors of Cinna, determined to keep him from entering Rome. Sulla decided to spend the remainder of that year, and most of the following one, consolidating support in central and southern Italy and waging a civil war against the consular armies. He was completely successful, and at the end of 82 B.C. he entered Rome and declared himself dictator. There followed another bloodbath, as Sulla rooted out all opposition. It was at this time that he exiled young Caesar for daring to defy him.

Sulla had also ordered another young man—Gnaeus Pompeius, better known to history as Pompey—to divorce his wife, who was from a Marian family. Unlike Caesar, Pompey obeyed, and he soon became Sulla's favorite assistant. During the following three years Pompey helped the dictator in his efforts to reform the government, and to return all political power to the hands of the Senate. When Sulla was satisfied that the Senate was again able to exercise supreme power, he resigned in 79 B.C., and the following year he died peacefully.

CHAPTER 2

Lawyer, Priest, Politician, Soldier?

The Early Career of Caesar

The family of Caius Julius Caesar traced its ancestry back to the Trojan hero Aeneas. In childhood, Caesar received a good education in both Greek and Latin. He grew tall and slender, with a fair complexion and dark piercing eyes. Although most of his family were conservative optimates, or patricians, he as a young man became a member of the liberal populares, or plebeian, party. He was perhaps influenced in this political affiliation by the fact that his aunt Julia was the wife of Marius.

After spending three years of exile in Asia, Caesar learned of Sulla's death and returned to Rome in 78 B.C. He thereupon set about establishing a reputation as an excellent lawyer. His eloquence made him very popular, and he was said to be second only to the great Cicero as an orator. In 75 B.C., Caesar went to Rhodes to study rhetoric under Cicero's former teacher.

It seems that during this trip to Rhodes, Caesar's ship was attacked by priates off the island of Pharmacussa (Fermaco), near Miletus, and he was taken captive. When the pirates demanded twenty talents* for ransom he laughed and told them it should be fifty talents. The pirates kept him for about six weeks while they waited for his ransom to come from Miletus. During his enforced stay he became friendly with the pirates, played games with them, and practiced his oratory. In apparent jest he said he would return to crucify them, the usual punishment for piracy. When his ransom finally came, Caesar was released at once. Going quickly to Miletus he procured some ships and some soldiers, then returned to the pirates' hideout. He took most of them prisoner, and recovered the ransom money. Then he proceeded to have them crucified as he had promised.

Caesar left Rhodes at the beginning of the Third Mithridatic War, in 74 B.C., and served in Caria as a junior officer. Then he returned to Rome, where he was elected to his first public office, that of military tribune. Very little is known of his life from that year, 73, to 69 B.C., when he was elected quaestor. But his aunt and his wife died shortly before he left for Further Spain, late in 69 B.C. to serve on the staff of the praetor, C. Antistius Vetus. It was while he was in Spain, that Plutarch tells us that Caesar saw a statue of Alexander the Great in the temple of Hercules at Gades (Cadiz). Caesar "sighed deeply, as if weary of his sluggish life, for having performed no memorable actions at an age at which Alexander had already conquered the world." It was still some years before he would make his mark on the world.

* The Attic talent was approximately 58 pounds in weight, worth about $835 in silver or $32,500 in gold (1967 prices). This ransom was probably in silver talents, and thus was probably about $16,700.

15

Returning to Rome, in 68 B.C., Caesar married the wealthy Pompeia, daughter of an aristocrat who had been killed by Marius, and granddaughter of Sulla himself. Whereas his first marriage had been for love, this one seems to have been for political convenience, since the populares were out of favor at the time.

The Rise of Pompey

Meanwhile Caesar's old friend Pompey had prospered greatly. After helping Sulla in Italy, in 78 B.C. Pompey had been sent to Sardinia and Africa, where supporters of Marius were instigating revolts. Shortly after Sulla's death Pompey was called back to Rome by the Senate to halt an attempt by M. Aemilius Lepidus to seize control. He suppressed the revolt, then went to Spain, where he put down another insurrection. He returned to Italy in 71 B.C., in time to help stamp out the uprising of slaves that Spartacus had initiated two years before.

Pompey and the other successful commander in the final campaign against the slaves, M. Licinius Crassus, were elected consuls, although both were opposed by the conservatives, the optimates. The two consuls then worked together to reduce the power of the Senate and to restore power to the populares.

While Crassus devoted himself to acquiring money and political power, Pompey returned to a military career. In 67 B.C. he organized a fleet and swept the many pirates from the

Mediterranean Sea. The following year he was sent to command in another war against Mithridates. Actually the war had already been won by other Roman generals, but Pompey drove Mithridates into exile. He then annexed Syria and Palestine to the Roman Empire, and during the next five years established new cities throughout the Eastern Mediterranean area.

Many Roman politicians were worried when Pompey returned to Rome in 61 B.C. He had been treated like an absolute monarch as he marched with his army through the East. When Pompey landed at Brundisium, however, far from taking advantage of his position of strength, he disbanded his army before proceeding to Rome, in a gesture to show his loyalty to the Senate. He soon regretted this, however, for without force to back him up he was unable to get the Senate to ratify the treaties he had made in the East, or to provide his soldiers with the land he had promised them. Although a good general, Pompey was not a skillful politician.

Caesar's Political Rise

Sometime after 66 B.C. Caesar had become allied with Crassus, who was jealous of Pompey's successes in the East and eager to win support of the populares. In 65 B.C., when Crassus was consul, Caesar was an aedile. Since one of his duties was to superintend public games, he proceeded to produce spectacular displays which won him the hearty support of the populace.

17

This was terribly expensive, but wealthy Crassus supplied much of the money.

Soon after this there was a vacancy in the office of *Pontifex Maximus*, the chief religious official of Rome. By persuading one of the tribunes to sponsor a bill making this lifetime office subject to popular election, and by generous use of money, Caesar secured the office. The expenses of this election, and his lavish popular entertainments, resulted in Caesar's going into debt, despite help from Crassus.

Caesar was made praetor in 62 B.C. During that year there occurred an incident that caused a great scandal. In the first week of December it was customary to hold a religious ceremony in honor of a Roman goddess known as Bona Dea. The rites were for women only and on this occasion were held in Caesar's house. As the ceremony was progressing, a young man, Publius Clodius, said to be the lover of Caesar's wife, was discovered among the women. A commission was appointed to try Clodius for sacrilege, and Caesar at once divorced his wife. However, he refused to testify against Clodius, who had political influence with Crassus. Because of insufficient evidence, and with the help of jurors bribed by Crassus, Clodius was acquitted. He remained grateful to Caesar.

Caesar had been awarded the propraetorship of Further Spain, but his departure for his post was delayed by the trial of Clodius and also by the demands of his creditors that he settle his tremendous debts before he left Rome. Crassus again came to his rescue, however, and by midsummer of 61 B.C. Caesar was in Spain.

18

Now, in his fortieth year, came Caesar's first opportunity to command an army. Further Spain was in turmoil because of tribal revolts. Unfortunately the ancient sources give little information on his campaigns in Spain. In any event he gave a good account of himself as a soldier and an administrator.

Caesar had in his command about 10,000 men. He first subdued the Lusitanians and the Callaeci, who had been causing trouble in the area between the Tagus and the Douro rivers. Driving the last of the enemy onto a coastal island, he sent to Gades for ships, which enabled him to take his men over to the island and subdue the fugitives. Then he sailed to Brigantium (Corunna), where the sight of his large fleet apparently was sufficiently impressive to cause the surrender of the inhabitants. Caesar's action seems to have resulted in the securing of approximately the area of modern Portugal for Rome. When his year in Spain ended, Caesar set sail for Rome late in 60 B.C.

CHAPTER 3

The First Triumvirate

Political Maneuvering

Having won a military victory, Caesar's next objective was to be elected to the highest position in Rome's Republican government, that of consul. Apparently he saw this as a step to a pro-consulship where he might win greater military success and prestige at least as great as that of Pompey. But first he was eager to receive the honor to which a victorious Roman general was entitled: the triumph.

This Roman institution, the highest honor a general could receive, was granted by vote of the Senate. Under Roman law a general could never bring an army into Rome. But during a triumph the general was accorded the privilege of entering the city without relinquishing command of his army. Led by the chief Roman officials and the members of the Senate, a solemn procession moved from the city gate to the Capitoline Hill. The procession also included trumpeters, booty taken in the war, pictures or models of the battles or the cities captured, sacrificial animals, and some prisoners. Then came the general himself, in robes of purple and gold, riding in a chariot, while a slave held the golden crown of Jupiter above his head. Finally came the soldiers of his army. At the Temple of Jupiter on the Capitoline the general placed a laurel branch in the lap of the statue and made sacrifices. Then came a great feast. It was an honor won by few generals, and one which Caesar was anxious to gain.

Caesar and his army arrived outside the city on the very day when candidates for the office of consul were required to present themselves and register their names in person in the city. But until the Senate voted him a triumph, he was forbidden to enter Rome as a general. Reluctant to relinquish his right to a triumph by setting foot within the city walls, Caesar asked the Senate to permit him to be represented by a proxy. But one of his political enemies was able to delay a vote, and at the end of the day Caesar was forced to make a choice. He gave up his hope for a triumph and presented himself as a candidate.

Caesar's election was certain, for he was very popular with the people of Rome. The conservatives, however, were able to elect one of his determined opponents, M. Calpurnius Bibulus, as the other consul. Then, in the pre-inauguration selection of provinces to be governed by the consuls after their year of office, Caesar was again outmaneuvered by his political enemies. The Senate assigned both consuls to the Civil Department of Forests and Cattle-Drifts. This assignment to supervise public lands in Italy greatly amused the citizens of Rome. It was not only a damaging political insult, it deprived Caesar of the opportunity of replenishing his purse which would have been offered by a rich provincial governorship. His opponents hoped in this way to ruin him both financially and politically.

Partnership of Pompey, Crassus, and Caesar

Caesar responded to these affronts by seeking political alliance with Pompey, whose prestige was still great. In return for Pompey's support, Caesar promised to secure approval of the treaties Pompey had made in the East and obtain from the Senate the land grants Pompey had promised his soldiers. He also gave Pompey the hand of his daughter Julia in marriage.

To increase the political strength he could muster against the leaders of the Senate, Caesar also enlisted the support of his old friend Crassus. Crassus had long been jealous of Pompey, and had now become jealous of Caesar as well. But he seems to have believed that he could play these two powerful men against each other. Thus was created what has come to be called the First Triumvirate: a powerful political alliance to which Pompey offered the army veterans, Crassus provided the money, and Caesar supplied the love and support of the populace.

Immediately upon taking office Caesar introduced a bill in the Senate to grant land for Pompey's veterans, and also to provide land to resettle some of the congested population of Rome. It was a reasonable bill, and since it involved mostly public land, it would not have required a very great expenditure from the treasury. The Senate, however, took no immediate action. Finally one of Caesar's political enemies, M. Porcius

Cato, spoke out at length against the bill. Caesar had him removed from the platform. When Cato's supporters objected, Caesar adjourned the Senate and took the bill to the Assembly. There Crassus and Pompey spoke in favor of it, and it was supported by a great majority of the Assembly; but when it was put to a vote it was vetoed by three tribunes. But such a veto could be overridden by another vote.

Now Caesar's co-consul, Bibulus, came to the support of the opposition. The Assembly could meet only if both of the consuls were able to announce that, through observation of good omens, the gods were favorable. Bibulus made it clear that he would prevent the Assembly from meeting for the rest of the year by refusing to report that the omens for a meeting were propitious. Caesar's reaction was to call in Pompey's veterans, many of whom were at hand in Rome, to drive his opponents from the Assembly. The law was quickly passed, with an additional clause requiring all senators to swear they would not resist it, on pain of exile.

Caesar next secured approval of Pompey's treaties in the East and also got a bill passed relieving Crassus of a heavy financial obligation. Then, for himself, Caesar persuaded the Assembly to set aside the Senate's earlier assignment of the cattle-drift province, and to assign to him instead the proconsulship of Cisalpine Gaul (northern Italy) and Illyricum. This was to be for five years instead of the usual two.

By chance, shortly after this, the governor of Transalpine Gaul (southeast France) died suddenly. At the recommendation of Pompey, the Senate, by now intimidated by the Triumvirate and by Caesar's display of power, awarded this province also to Caesar. No doubt there were many senators who recognized the advantage of removing Caesar from Rome for five years, with the possibility that he might suffer a humiliating defeat in his attempt to control this large area, bordered as it was by unruly barbarian tribes.

During the remainder of his year in office, Caesar established his friends in official positions in order to make sure that his influence in Rome would remain strong while he was absent. He and Pompey selected the consuls for the following year, and Caesar married the daughter of one of these consuls, L. Calpurnius Piso. To frustrate opposition he also secured the support of Publius Clodius, the same man who had been accused of desecration of the rites of Bona Dea, and the apparent lover of Caesar's former wife. He arranged for the election of Clodius as tribune. In this sensitive position Clodius succeeded in removing Caesar's two strongest opponents, Cicero and Cato, from Rome. Cicero was forced to go into exile, and Cato was appointed governor of Cyprus. Temporarily at least the Triumvirate was secure from its political enemies.

CHAPTER 4

The Conquest of Gaul

Troubles in Gaul

Transalpine Gaul had been made a Roman province in 120 B.C. In following years trade had flourished throughout the colony. By the time Caesar arrived, the Province, as it was known, had been well Romanized and its people had become completely loyal to Rome.

North and west beyond the Province, independent or outer Gaul included all of modern France and those parts of Holland, Belgium, and Switzerland west of the Rhine River. The area was apparently well-populated, inhabited by at least 10 million people and perhaps as many as 20 million. Most of the Gauls were semi-civilized, living in small villages. There were about 200 or 300 tribes, each with its own special form of government, and each belonging to one of about 20 loose national tribal confederations. Largely on the basis of language differences, by the first century B.C. there were three principal groups of tribes in Gaul: the Celts, or Gauls, who lived in the center, the Aquitani in the south and southwest, and the Belgae in the north and northeast.

25

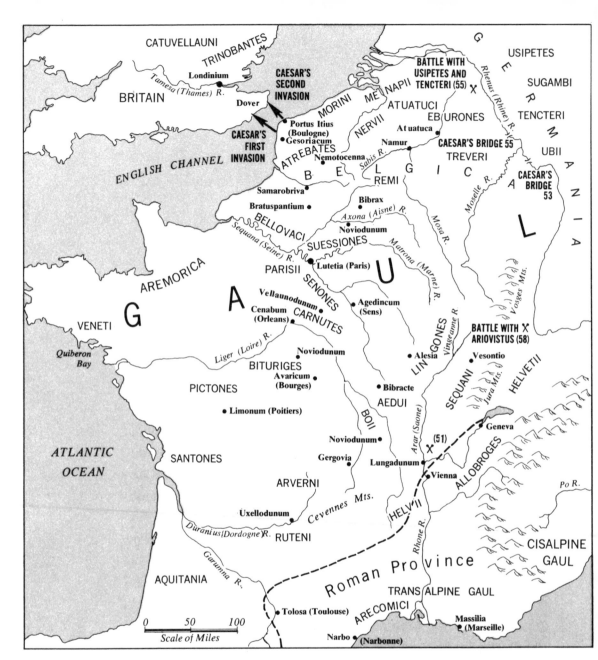

The Campaigns in Gaul.

Rome had had little official contact with outer Gaul, except for a treaty in 123 B.C. recognizing as friends and allies of the Roman people the Aedui, a group of Celtic tribes who lived in the region between the upper Seine River and the Vosges Mountains. In 121 B.C. Rome intervened in their behalf against the Arverni from Auvergne.

In 71 B.C. or later the Arverni joined the Sequani, another Celtic people, in an attempt to overcome the Aedui. The allies received help from Ariovistus, chieftain of a Germanic tribe from east of the Rhine, who thereupon compelled the Sequani to give him Alsace in return for his assistance. The Sequani then changed sides to join the Aedui in fighting Ariovistus, and both tribes were defeated decisively by the Germans and Arverni. The Aedui appealed to Rome for help, but received no response.

At about the same time, some of the Aedui tribes sought the help of the Helvetii, a warlike people who lived in roughly the territory of modern Switzerland. There the Aeduan emissaries met with greater success. An attack on Ariovistus seemed to work in well with a plan already being considered by the Helvetii. They had been under increasing pressure from German tribes to the north, and were planning to move west into the region between the Liger (Loire) and the Garumna (Garonne) rivers.

In 59 B.C. Ariovistus sought Roman recognition of his rights in Gaul and sent envoys to Rome. Caesar was consul at the time and seems to have furthered the recognition of Ariovistus by the Senate as "king and friend of the Roman people." Unfortunately we do not know why Caesar and other Romans made this decision to recognize the enemy of their Aeduan allies.

Caesar did not leave Rome at once upon the expiration of his term as consul. He was still there in mid-March when word came that the Helvetii were mustering on the north side of the Rhone, near Geneva, preparing to cross the northern portion of the Roman Province on their way to southwestern Gaul. Losing no time, Caesar headed for Geneva.

At this time there was only one Roman legion in Transalpine Gaul. Starting with that single legion, Caesar built up an army with which eventually he conquered all of Gaul. In order to understand fully his military campaigns, it will be useful to re-view the organization and appearance of the Roman army of the time.

Roman Military Organization

The consular legions of the Republican period before the time of Marius comprised 4,200 infantry and 300 cavalry. Four of these legions were raised annually in Rome. The same number of infantrymen plus twice as many cavalry were required to be furnished by the allied cities and tribes of Italy.

The heavy infantry of the legion was organized in three lines. The youngest troops made up the *hastati*, in front. Behind them came more experienced veterans, the *principes*. The oldest troops, the *triarii*, were in the third line. In each legion there

28

Viletes were light Roman infantrymen.

was usually 1,200 hastati and 1,200 principes, plus 600 triarii. The remaining 1,200 soldiers were from the poorest citizens, who served as light infantry, and were known as *velites*. In addition there were usually a few hundred *fabri*, skilled artisans who repaired arms and armor and who supervised construction. The fabri were usually stout fighters, available for combat when not actually working at their crafts.

Each line of the legion was divided in ten units, or *maniples*, thirty in all. Each maniple of the hastati and principes consisted of two *centuries*, commanded by centurions; the senior centurion commanded the maniple. In the triarii each century formed for battle as a separate maniple.

29

A Roman horseman.

The heavy infantrymen carried semi-cylindrical, rectangular shields made of wood and canvas or leather, rimmed with iron and with a metal boss in the center. They wore mail, or brass, helmet and breastplate and carried a 2-foot-long, two-edged Spanish sword, two javelins, and a dagger. The javelins were about 6 feet long and had barbed heads. The triarii carried long spears instead of javelins. The unarmored velites carried swords, two javelins, and a round shield 3 feet in diameter. They wore wolf's-skin hats instead of helmets.

The legionary cavalry was divided in two squadrons, each commanded by a *decurio*. The horsemen wore armor and helmets and carried shield, spears, and swords. The Roman cavalrymen relied on their horses mainly for transportation; they ordinarily fought on foot.

A Roman legionary.

Marius, in addition to creating a professional army by abolishing the landowning requirement, increased the number of infantry in each legion to 6,000 and divided the legion into ten *cohorts*, each consisting of three maniples; the cohorts then became the tactical units of the legion. (There is some evidence that the cohorts had been a part of the organization for many years before Marius.) The cohorts were usually deployed in three lines, with four cohorts in the first and three in the second and the third.

There is no evidence that Caesar did much to change the Marian army, except for increasing discipline and improving morale. Like his predecessors he did nothing to improve the weakest element of the Roman army, the cavalry. He followed

A Gallic horseman.

the example of Marius and Sulla, and hired foreign horsemen. At the outset of his first Gallic campaign he had about 4,000 Gallic horsemen, mostly raised from the Aedui and their allies.

Roman and Gallic Tactics

In the typical Roman three-line formation, the front line was engaged first with the enemy, while the second remained behind, ready to move in which needed to reinforce or replace the first. The third line was held as reserves farther back, in order to support the front lines as needed or to move in at the climax of a battle to clinch a victory with fresh troops.

The Romans habitually went into battle with much larger intervals between men than was the case of any other army of antiquity. This gave each soldier better opportunity to wield his weapons. By the first century B.C., the Romans seem to have abandoned their earlier *quincunx*, or checkerboard disposition of cohorts and maniples.

The Gauls, who were to be Caesar's first important adversaries, had no strict organization and little discipline. They believed that the greater the number of men the more effective. They charged in large masses, wielding their great cutting swords, and yelling at the top of their lungs. It was a terrifying sight, and the more civilized Romans were easily intimidated by the ferocious Gauls. But the force of training and discipline usually enabled the Roman legion to stand firm. Rarely had a Gallic army defeated a Roman force, since a disaster at Arausio, in 105 B.C.

Migration of the Helvetii

It was in 60 B.C. that the Helvetii had finally decided to escape the German hordes pressing in from the east and north by migrating to western Gaul. According to Caesar, there were 92,000 fighting Helvetii men, and 276,000 more women, children, and old men. Even if these figures are exaggerated, it represented a tremendous movement and required preparation. Two years, in fact, were spent by the Helvetii in collecting food and transportation, before the migration began.

There were two routes available to the Helvetii: The southern route led from Geneva by way of the territory of the Allobroges and the Roman Province; the other was more difficult, between the Jura Mountains and the Rhone and through the territory of the Sequani. Early in 58 B.C., therefore, the Helvetii sent envoys to request permission to pass through the Roman Province. Caesar put off the decision until April 13, and used the time to raise more soldiers and to build a chain of fortifications about 18 miles long, across the upper Rhone Valley. When the envoys returned he refused the permission. Some attempts to break through the Roman defense were repulsed by the single legion Caesar had available.

The Helvetii next approached the Sequani, who gave them the permission they sought. This route would take them away from Roman territory, and unless they became involved with the Aedui, Rome would have no formal justification for doing anything further about it. Caesar, however, feared that the move of the Helvetii would put them in a position to threaten the Province from the northwest. He decided to oppose the planned migration.

Operations Against the Helvetii

Leaving Titus Labienus, his second-in-command, in charge of the Rhone fortifications, Caesar went to Cisalpine Gaul to enroll two new legions. With these and three that were already there he rushed back. Joined by Labienus and his legion, he crossed the Rhone, heading north, his total force probably slightly less than 40,000 men. At this time envoys from the Aedui reached Caesar, reporting that the Helvetii were already ravaging their territory, and asking Caesar's help.

This gave Caesar a legal basis for action. He marched quickly north with three legions, the other three following behind. He surprised the Helvetii, just as they were crossing the Arar (Saône) River, and wiped out their rear guard—probably about 20,000 men—who were still on the eastern side of the river. He then crossed the river and hurried after the main body of the Helvetii, who were moving slowly north up the river valley.

Ahead of his legions Caesar sent his cavalry, about 4,000 in all. They proved useless, however, being driven back in a skirmish with 500 Helvetian horsemen. For about two weeks Caesar followed a few miles behind the enemy. He made one attempt to attack a portion of the Helvetii host, but this failed through the mistake of a subordinate.

Supply was becoming a critical problem for the Romans, partly because some of the Aedui failed to cooperate as requested. So Caesar decided to turn off toward Bibracte (near Autun), capital of the Aedui, to procure supplies. As soon as they detected this move, the Helvetii also changed their direction to try to head off the Romans, and attacked the Roman rear guard. Caesar sent his cavalry to support the rear guard, and meanwhile deployed his four veteran legions on the western slope of some hills near Armecy. The Helvetii left their noncombatants in an encampment, or laager, ringed by wagons. They pressed after the Roman rear guard and cavalry, advancing "in a densely crowded line."

The Romans stood their ground as the horde rushed upon them. Just before the leading Gauls reached their line, the principes hurled their javelins. Many Helvetii were cut down, and others had to drop their shields, since the javelins stuck in them, making them unwieldy. In the hand-to-hand fighting that followed, the Helvetii were finally driven back. As they withdrew, the Romans advanced.

Suddenly some 15,000 of the foe swooped down in a surprise attack upon the Roman right flank. Caesar's men were forced to halt to deal with this threat, and at that moment the retreating Helvetii rushed back and again attacked on the Roman front. But the legions stood firm, and again the barbarians were repulsed. This time they withdrew to their encampment, to take refuge within the circle of wagons. Fighting there continued after darkness fell, with the Gallic warriors supported by women and children. Finally the Romans prevailed and broke through into the camp, slaughtering the panic-stricken defenders. The surviving Helvetii (Caesar says 130,000) fled, leaving most of their wagons and their other possessions behind them.

Caesar rested his men for three days before pursuing. By then the Helvetii were ready to surrender. They were out of food, and Caesar had persuaded the nearby Gauls not to let them have supplies. A few who tried to ecape to the Rhine were captured and sold into slavery. At the request of the Aedui, one tribe of Helvetian allies—the Boii—was given farmland in their territory. Caesar ordered the remainder to return to their homeland, where they henceforth served as a buffer between the Germans and the Allobroges and the Roman Province.

The German Threat

Caesar's success against the Helvetii gave him great prestige throughout Gaul. From tribes from far and wide came representatives to offer their congratulations. A number of the Celtic chieftains held a meeting and appointed the Aeduan chief, Divitiacus, as their spokesman to beg Caesar to become their protector, and to drive Ariovistus and his Germans out of Gaul. Already there were about 120,000 Germans in Alsace, and more Germans seemed ready to pour across the Rhine. They had driven out thousands of Sequani from their homes, and threatened to extend their conquest to all of Gaul. Caesar agreed to help the Gauls, and then sought a means of carrying out his promise, for he had himself approved the naming of Ariovistus "king and friend of the Roman people."

Caesar's first move was to send an envoy, suggesting a meeting with the German chieftain. When this was rejected by Ariovistus, Caesar sent a firm message, pointing out that the Roman Senate had directed him to protect the Aedui and other friends of Rome. Hence he could not overlook their suffering at the hands of Ariovistus. No more Germans would be permitted to cross the Rhine, and the hostages Ariovistus had taken from the Aedui must be returned. In response, Ariovistus called on his rights as a conqueror and warned that no one had fought Ariovistus without being destroyed.

At this same time Caesar learned that many Germans were assembling on the east bank of the Rhine, threatening to cross and reinforce Ariovistus. Caesar decided to act. By forced marches he moved his army to the Sequani's largest town, Vesontio (Besançon), where he paused to consolidate supplies. The natives were so full of tales of German barbarities that many of Caesar's men were frightened, and the threat of mutiny spread through his legions.

Caesar summoned his officers and reprimanded them. He pointed out that they had already beaten the Helvetii, who often had fought and overcome Germans. If everyone else was unwilling to accompany him, he said, he would go with the 10th Legion alone, for he had complete confidence in its fidelity. The men of the 10th were pleased, and formed up for the march at once. The rest fell in behind. His army intact, Caesar continued on his way.

A week later, when Caesar's army was about 20 miles from Ariovistus' camp, the German leader sent messengers to tell Caesar that he was willing to meet. He suggested that each commander should bring with him only a mounted escort. Caesar had learned that his allied horsemen were not very trustworthy, and he also realized that this was well known to Ariovistus. So he mounted the 10th Legion and took it along as an escort. The two leaders, each accompanied by ten horsemen, met on a knoll, having left their mounted escorts 200 paces away.

When Caesar repeated his earlier ultimatum, Ariovistus replied that he had arrived in central Gaul before the Romans. He said that he intended to remain. He knew enough about polities in Rome, furthermore, to realize that if he killed Caesar he would win the friendship and gratitude of many Romans. If Caesar would leave him alone, however, he would assist Caesar against his enemies in Italy and in Gaul.

Caesar disputed Ariovistus' claim to central Gaul. He said that by defeating the Arverni in 121 B.C. the Romans had acquired exclusive claim to all of Gaul. At this point a Roman soldier rode up and told Caesar that some of the German horsemen were throwing stones and darts. Caesar immediately broke off the meeting and returned to his camp.

Operations Against Ariovistus

Two days later Ariovistus moved his forces around and past the Roman camp to establish a fortified camp where it could cut off Caesar's communications with Vesontio. For five days Caesar tried in vain to tempt Ariovistus to fight. Then in order to open his communications route he built a smaller camp south of the Germans and placed in it two legions and some of his auxiliaries. On the following day Ariovistus attacked the new camp but was driven off.

The next morning Caesar placed all his allied troops in front of the smaller camp, and with his six legions in a triple line he marched right up to the main German camp. Ariovistus was

39

no longer able to ignore the challenge. He formed his army by tribes, seven of them, and placed the wagons and the women and children behind. Caesar, noting that the German left wing seemed less steady than the right or center, took command of his own right. Both armies rushed toward each other, so rapidly that the Romans could not hurl their javelins but closed with their swords.

The German left wing was soon torn to shreds. The right wing, however, was making progress against the Roman left when a cavalry commander, young Publius Crassus, son of the Triumvir, ordered up the third line. The Germans were repulsed, then they broke and fled, not stopping until they reached the Rhine 15 miles away. There most of them fell victim to the pursuing Roman cavalry, although a few managed to swim across the river. Ariovistus himself escaped in a boat, only to die shortly afterward. This decisive defeat dissuaded any more Germans from crossing into Gaul.

Victorious Caesar returned to Vesontio, where he put his men into winter quarters. All of the Celtic tribes of Central Gaul now acknowledged Caesar as their protector. Leaving Labienus in command, Caesar returned to Cisalpine Gaul to carry out his provincial duties and to regain contact with Rome.

The Belgae Prepare for War

While Caesar was in the south, reports arrived that the Belgae were fearful that, like the Celtic Gauls, they would soon be absorbed into the Roman Province. They were apparently encouraged to plot against Rome by some of the Celtic Gauls who did not like losing their authority in their own land. Caesar raised two more legions and sent them in the spring to join the others at Vesontio. He soon followed them.

Caesar waited long enough to confirm the rumors that the Belgae were in fact preparing for war, and to procure supplies for his forces. Then, with 40,000 men, he set out for the Belgic frontier on the Matrona (Marne) River. He was accompanied by a force of Aeduans under Divitiacus. Within two weeks he had reached the edge of the territory of the Remi, one of the Belgic tribes. The Remi had not joined the others in mobilizing and now eagerly sought Roman protection. In return they furnished Caesar with much information on the strength and organization of the other Belgae. Fifteen Belgic tribes, totaling about 300,000 warriors, were allied under the overall command of Galba, king of the Suessiones.

To divide his enemy, Caesar asked Divitiacus to take the Aeduans into the territory of the Bellovaci, farther west (near Beauvais). By laying waste the area, they might succeed in drawing the Bellovaci—who reportedly had about 100,000 fighting men—away from the main campaign.

Campaign Against the Belgae

Caesar then learned that the Belgae were in fact moving toward him. He crossed the Axona (Aisne) River, probably at modern Berry-au-Bac, leaving a strong garrison to hold the bridge. With his supply route secure and the river at his back, he built a strongly fortified camp in the customary Roman fashion, 8 miles from the Remi's chief town, Bibrax.

The Belgae, desiring vengeance against the Remi for their defection to Caesar, first attacked Bibrax, whose defenders barely succeeded in holding out until nightfall. When Caesar received a message asking for help, he sent a detachment of Numidian and Cretan archers and some Balearic slingers to harass the attackers. This quickly caused the Belgae to turn their attention against the Romans. They abandoned the attempt to take Bibrax, and after devastating the countryside, they moved up to within 2 miles of the Roman camp. Their watchfires, wrote Caesar, showed that their camp extended over a front of more than 8 miles.

Caesar was reluctant to attack the Belgae. He was impressed by their numbers and by the reports he had heard of their prowess as warriors. But, after a few cavalry skirmishes in which his men proved themselves at least the equal of the enemy, he decided to risk a battle. The Belgae also drew up their forces. But neither side would move to cross the marshes that separated the two armies and consequently there was no action.

Next, some of the Belgae managed to cross the Axona with the obvious intention of attacking the six cohorts Caesar had left to guard the bridge. Taking his cavalry and some Numidian light troops, slingers, and archers, he crossed the bridge and advanced to meet the Belgae as they forded the river a few miles away. There was a fierce fight and the Belgae abandoned the attempt.

The Belgae then held a council of war. Since they could not

agree on a course of action, they decided that it would be better to fight in friendly territory. They agreed that all should return home and reassemble in whatever areas the Romans decided to invade. The Bellovaci had already decided to go, for word had reached them that the Aeduans were plundering their territory. So, in the dark of the night, the Belgic camp was broken up, and all started for home in complete disorganization, each eager to get home first. Caesar waited to be sure that it was not a trick and then sent his cavalry and three legions to pursue them for a day. The Romans caught up with the rear guard and mangled it a bit, turning the withdrawal into a confused rout.

Caesar set out the following day with his whole army to take advantage of this development. Marching rapidly into the territory of the Suessiones, he attacked the town of Noviodunum (Pommiers). The appearance of Roman siege towers, a sight never before seen in the region, was enough to convince the defenders to yield. Their surrender included the whole tribe, and two sons of Galba were among the hostages given to the Romans as evidence of good faith.

From there Caesar headed for the land of the Bellovaci. While he was still 5 miles from their chief fortress, Bratuspantium, emissaries came to say they would not resist. Caesar accepted the surrender and promised to spare them destruction. He took all their weapons, and claimed 600 hostages, since they were the largest and most powerful of the Belgic tribes. Caesar next marched to the territory of the Nervii, said to be the fiercest of all the Belgae. As the Romans approached the

43

Sabis (Sambre) River, Caesar learned that the Nervii, together with the Atrebates and the Viromandui, were awaiting him across the river. Marching at the head of six lightly equipped legions, Caesar selected a site for a camp on a hill that rose from the riverbank. He set his men to work to dig trenches and cut timber to fortify the camp.

Unbeknown to Caesar, some of the subdued Belgae who were accompanying his army had gone ahead and informed the Nervii of his approach. He was accustomed, they reported, to place a transport column behind each legion as he marched. Consequently the first legion could be easily ambushed, and following legions—isolated from each other by supply wagons—would not attempt to make a stand.

The Nervii adopted this suggestion, but this time Caesar had brought on six legions ahead of the supply trains. However, he was apparently not aware of the proximity of the enemy, and he neglected to maintain part of his men under arms while the remainder worked on the fortifications.

Battle of the Sabis

When the transport train came in sight, the Nervii rushed out thinking they would be opposed by only one legion. They drove the Roman cavalry off in confusion and then swarmed across the river and up the hill toward the Roman camp so fast that there was no time to prepare for this attack. Fortunately the training and experience of the Roman soldiers and their officers served them well. The men fell in with the first unit they encountered, rather than searching for their own. The legions formed to meet the attack with no time for tactical planning or organization. Caesar left the individual formations to his legionary commanders and himself rode down the line, giving encouragement and issuing essential orders.

The 9th and 10th Legions, at the left of the Roman line, were attacked by the Atrebates, who arrived breathless from their rapid advance, to be met by a hail of Roman javelins. They fell back, pursued by the Romans who drove them across the river and then broke up a stand on the slope on the opposite bank. Next to the 10th, at a different angle, the 11th and 8th Legions encountered the Viromandui, whom they also drove down to the river.

On the right, the 12th and 7th Legions were close together. The advance of the other legions left these two isolated, and exposed the front and left of the half-built camp. The Nervii swarmed up the hill in a mass. Some of them enveloped the two legions; others headed for the camp. Chaos ensued. The Roman cavalry fled, auxiliaries of all types broke and ran, camp followers and the baggage train ran off in all directions, and some Gallic cavalry rushed home to spread the word that the Roman army had been destroyed.

Caesar, pleased with the success of his left and center, rode up and found to his dismay that his right flank was close to defeat. The men of the 12th Legion were huddled together, many officers were dead or wounded, and the legionaries were so closely packed that they were scarcely able to wield a sword,

45

while the enemy closed in on both flanks. Seizing a shield from a man in the rear, Caesar rode out in front of the demoralized legion. He ordered the ranks to open up so that the men could swing their swords, and urged them to resist the enemy attack. He ordered the 7th Legion to join the 12th to form a single square, fighting back to back, so that each supported the other.

At this point the two legions that had been the rear guard, protecting the transport column, appeared and rushed up to help. Labienus, who had captured the Nervii camp on the opposite side of the river, also saw the situation near the Roman camp. He sent the 10th Legion back to the rescue. The arrival of these reinforcements revived the spirits of the hard-pressed legionaries, and inspired the cavalry to return to the fray. The Belgae fought viciously but were cut to pieces.

"This engagement brought the name and nation of the Nervii almost to utter destruction," said Caesar. The older men, women, and children sent envoys to offer surrender, reporting that of a national council of 600 men only 3 survived and that their military force of 60,000 had been reduced to about 500. Caesar showed clemency to the survivors, confirming their territorial rights and warning the neighboring tribes that they must leave the Nervii alone.

Completing the Belgic Campaign

The Atuatuci, who lived north of the Nervii, were on their way to help when this fierce struggle was taking place. They returned to their own territory and concentrated in one of their fortified towns, well defended by steep, rocky cliffs except for a 200-foot-wide approach up a slope. When the Romans erected siege towers and started to move them close to the city walls, however, the people surrendered. Caesar ordered them to surrender their weapons, but they hid many. That evening, rearmed, they tried unsuccessfully to storm the Roman camp. The Romans quickly overwhelmed them. This time Caesar was not lenient, but sold the entire population into slavery.

This ended Caesar's campaigning for the year 57 B.C. After the Battle of the Sabis, Caesar had sent Publius Crassus with the 7th Legion to conquer the Veneti and other tribes in Normandy and Brittany. He soon received word from Crassus that the entire region had submitted.

Caesar had now brought under Roman control all of Gaul between the Garumna and the Rhine, except for the territory of the Morini and the Menapii in the north. His reputation as a victorious general caused German tribes from beyond the Rhine to send offers of submission. But Caesar dismissed them and asked them to return the following year. He was anxious to return to check on affairs in his other provinces of Cisalpine Gaul and Illyricum, and did not wish to engage in negotiations. As soon as his legions had gone into winter quarters on the Liger and the Sequana (Seine) he started for Italy. When word of Caesar's victories reached Rome he was awarded an unprecedented honor. Fifteen days of thanksgiving were decreed.

47

Caesar was still on his way south when he received a message from Crassus, which made it clear that there would be more fighting in Gaul the following year. After Crassus had overcome the Veneti, apparently Caesar had sent him to explore the coast of Britain. In any case the Veneti, who were a maritime people and had a monopoly on trade across the Channel with Britain, were fearful of the possibility of Roman competition.

Crassus had put his troops in winter quarters near the lower Liger River, in an area where there was insufficient grain to feed his men and horses. Consequently he sent envoys to the Veneti and the other tribes in the vicinity to secure grain. The Gauls held these envoys and sent word to Crassus that if he would restore the hostages they had recently given him, they would send back the Roman envoys.

When he learned about this, Caesar sent word to Crassus to have some ships built and gather crews for them. He knew he would have to smash the opposition of these seafaring people at sea. When spring came, Caesar hurried back to Gaul, and with his other legions he joined Crassus near the Liger.

To protect his line of communications, and maintain peace elsewhere, Caesar sent Labienus with some cavalry to the land of the Treveri, which bordered on the Rhine. He sent Crassus with twelve cohorts and some cavalry to Aquitania on the pretext of preventing the Aquitanians from sending reinforcements to northern Gaul. Quintus Titurius Sabinus was sent with three legions to subdue the tribes in northern Brittany and Nor-

48

mandy. Decimus Brutus was put in command of the new fleet, assembled between the Garumna and the Liger. Caesar himself would lead the remaining troops in an invasion of the Veneti lands.

Along the coast of Brittany the Veneti had built strongholds on small peninsulas whose connections with the mainland were underwater at high tide. Caesar managed to capture a few of these places by building walls that permitted his soldiers to cross at any tide. Then, from these walls, the Romans could attack the city walls from positions of equal or greater height. He found, however, that once this difficult and costly operation was completed the inhabitants simply brought boats up to the far side of the city and sailed away to another position. Realizing that this sort of campaign was accomplishing little, Caesar decided to wait for the arrival of Decimus Brutus and the Roman fleet.

Naval Actions on the Atlantic Coast

The Roman vessels were the typical galleys used in the Mediterranean. These vessels had fairly deep keels, and were propelled by oars, which gave them their one advantage over the ships of the Veneti: speed.

The Veneti had big, almost flat-bottomed sailing vessels made of oak. These boats drew so little water that they were not bothered by shallows or shoals, and could even rest on their bottoms when the tide went out. They were so high that the Romans could scarcely reach their decks with missiles or grapples, and the sturdy oak sides were not affected by the rams on the prows of the Roman vessels. They were propelled by leather sails suspended from a yard, probably not unlike those of the Vikings of later centuries.

Unable to deal with these ships otherwise, the Romans equipped themselves with long hooked poles. With these they grabbed the halyards of the Veneti's ships, pulled them taut, then rowed away, pulling until the halyards snapped and the sails fell uselessly to the decks.

With Caesar's men lining the shore of Quiberon Bay, Brutus and his fleet sailed up to challenge the Veneti. The Veneti sent 220 ships sailing out to meet the Romans. The halyard-snapping device worked. The Roman galleys rowed alongside the big Veneti ships, the halyards were grabbed and cut, and the sails fell to the decks. Then Roman troops swarmed aboard. Without oars, the Veneti could not move once their sails were gone, and they could devise no defense against this novel weapon. The remaining Veneti vessels tried to flee, only to be caught in a dead calm, which gave the Romans the opportunity to board almost every ship and so to destroy the Veneti as a maritime power. The only possible move was surrender.

Caesar was determined to make an example of these people and show all Gauls that the international laws respecting the rights of envoys must be observed. He had all the members of the Veneti's national council put to death. The rest of the people were sold as slaves.

This victory over the Veneti, and a successful campaign by

Crassus in Aquitania, won for the Romans control of the Bay of Biscay and the English Channel. But the ports nearest to Britain were still held by the Morini and the Menapii, who had resisted Sabinus' efforts to subjugate them. It was late in the summer when the Veneti campaign was concluded, but Caesar set out to march the 400 miles to the land of the Morini.

The Morini refused to fight, however, taking to the forests and waging a guerrilla-type warfare with which Caesar could not cope. He burned a few of their villages and devastated the land. When heavy fall rains began he abandoned the campaign and took his legions to winter quarters in the area of the Sequana and the Liger. Then he himself returned to Cisalpine Gaul as usual.

Germanic Invasion of Gaul

Once again trouble brewed while Caesar was away. Two German tribes, the Usipetes and Tencteri, had been forced from their land east of the Rhine by the Suebi. After wandering for some time, they crossed the Rhine and occupied land that belonged to the Menapii. Caesar rightly suspected that some of the Gallic tribes would welcome these invaders, who might help them fight against Rome.

Hurrying back to Gaul, early in 55 B.C., Caesar procured some cavalry and gathered supplies, then set out for the area where the Germans were reported to be. On the way he was met by envoys from the two tribes, offering friendship and pointing

51

out that they had come to Gaul because they had been forced out of their own territory. They asked a grant of land or permission to retain what they had taken. The Suebi, they admitted, had defeated them, but there was no one else on earth whom they could not conquer.

Caesar replied that he could not accept their friendship as long as they stayed in Gaul. He would, however, ask the Ubii, the only German tribe which was subject to Rome, to give them land east of the Rhine on which to settle. The envoys asked for three days in which to consult their chiefs and requested Caesar to advance no farther. He refused, suspecting that they were really playing for time until their cavalry, which was off foraging, could return.

When the German envoys returned, the Romans had advanced to within about 10 miles of their camp. Again the Germans asked Caesar to move no farther, in order that they might have three days in which to ask the Ubii if they might move into their land. Again Caesar was suspicious, but he agreed to advance only 3 or 4 miles, to the next river. Expecting treachery, he prepared to meet it with treachery of his own if necessary. He asked them to return the following day, bringing as many of their leaders as possible for a discussion. He instructed the commanders of his cavalry, who rode ahead, not to engage the enemy unless attacked. If they were attacked, they were to hold out until he could come up with the army.

Aware that the Germans were negotiating for peace, the 5,000 Gallic horsemen of Caesar's army were riding along casually, suspecting nothing and apparently watching for nothing, when 800 German cavalrymen suddenly swooped down upon them. The Gauls fled in panic, leaving 74 dead behind.

Caesar interpreted this action as a declaration of war, and began to prepare for battle. The following day a large number of Germans, including all their leaders and older men, appeared in Caesar's camp. He was overjoyed that they should so play into his hands. Placing the group under arrest, he set off with his whole army and surprised the Germans by appearing suddenly outside their camp, 8 miles away.

With all their chiefs in Caesar's hands, and no time to make plans or even prepare themselves to fight, the Germans panicked. The Roman soldiers poured into the camp, slaughtering men, women, and children. Those who fled were pursued and cut down. Some got to the river only to drown in its waters. According to Caesar the two tribes had numbered 430,000, probably an exaggeration. Virtually none survived the wholesale butchery. Caesar then permitted the leaders to leave, but they preferred to stay with the Romans rather than risk the wrath of the Gauls whose lands they had recently ravaged.

This deliberate slaughter is considered by most historians as Caesar's most disgraceful action. In light of the treacherous ambush of his troops the previous day, Caesar certainly had reason to punish the Germans. This cannot, however, justify wholesale massacre.

The cavalry of the Usipetes and Tencteri, which had been off foraging at the time of the massacre, had taken refuge with the Sugambri, north of modern Cologne. Caesar had demanded the surrender of the fugitive horsemen, but the Sugambri refused to surrender them. He decided to show the Germans that the Rhine was no obstacle to the power of Rome and prepared to cross the river. He felt this would also discourage the Germans from crossing into Gaul. Furthermore, the Ubii had invited him to visit them, since his appearance in their territory would be evidence of their friendship with Rome.

In ten days Caesar's men built a bridge across the Rhine, a tremendous engineering feat. He crossed with his army, to find that the Sugambri had fled into a densely forested area where he did not wish to follow. He devastated their lands and burned down their towns, then went to the land of the Ubii. There he affirmed the support of Rome to the Ubii in case of attack by the Suebi. The Suebi, he found, had also left their homes and concealed women and children in the woods. The fighting men were awaiting him, prepared for battle. Caesar ignored them, and did not attempt to enter Suebian territory. After a brief stay with the Ubii, he led his army back across the bridge, and destroyed it behind him.

In mid-August of 55 B.C., Caesar left the Rhine and marched west into the territory of the Morini. His objective was Britain, then little known and therefore intriguing to a man of Caesar's keen intellectual curiosity. According to his *Commentaries*, his excuse for going to Britain was that help from there had been coming to the Gauls. With the Channel and the Channel coast in Roman control, such help would cease, however. So it is more likely that Caesar was merely curious. Furthermore, he knew that even visiting the island would add to his prestige, and he hoped it would produce valuable booty. He sent a trusted officer ahead to find out what he could about harbors and about the native tribes.

Although the Morini had previously been unfriendly, Caesar wished to use the ports in their territory because they were closest to Britain. Fortunately his reputation had reached most of the Morini and they offered him hostages and submitted to Rome, thus securing his base in Gaul. Nevertheless, Caesar left a sizable force to guard the harbor of Gesoviacum, probably Boulogne. He also sent Sabinus and Aurunculeins Cotta with several legions to take care of the Menapii, and those tribes of the Morini who had not submitted.

At midnight on August 25 the expedition sailed, the 7th and 10th Legions in 80 transports. Their horses were embarked separately, but were unable to sail because of adverse winds. At 9 A.M. the first ships arrived off Dover, to see the cliffs ringed with armed natives. After waiting for the rest of the fleet to arrive, Caesar moved about 8 miles along to a sloping beach beyond Walmer. There the Romans landed, against stiff opposition from British cavalry and charioteers. The Britons were finally driven off and Caesar regretted the lack of cavalry with which to pursue them. Soon British envoys returned and asked for peace, giving hostages and promising more.

The cavalry transports appeared offshore four days later, but before they could land, a storm came up and drove them back out to sea. In disarray they returned to Gaul. That night most of Caesar's ships were damaged, blown ashore, smashed against each other, or sunk by an unusually high tide and big waves.

This disaster and the failure of the cavalry to land created near panic in the Roman camp. It also encouraged the Britons to try once more to drive the invaders out. They attacked twice but were driven off. After the second repulse they again sued for peace. Caesar demanded twice as many hostages and told them to deliver them on the Continent. He was anxious to leave before the weather worsened. He was also undoubtedly too short of transport space to carry them along on his own ships.

Most of the Roman ships had by this time been repaired, and Caesar left Britain, having accomplished little. Three hundred of his men were driven by the wind to land some distance from Boulogne. On their way to join the main body they were attacked by some of the Morini and had to be resuced by Caesar's cavalry. He then sent Labienus with the two recently returned legions to subdue the Morini.

Caesar put his legions in winter quarters in the territory of the Belgae. After leaving instructions to build as many ships as possible during the winter, Caesar once more returned to Italy.

Second Expedition to Britain

Before Caesar could embark on the invasion of Britain the following year, he found it necessary to take four legions and some 800 horsemen into the territory of the Treveri, who were showing signs of revolt and were negotiating with the Germans on the other side of the Rhine. He found that two of the Treveri chiefs, Indutiomarus and Cingetorix, were contending for tribe leadership. Cingetorix approached Caesar as soon as the Roman legions arrived and protested his loyalty. Indutiomarus, impressed by the show of force, also acknowledged Roman authority, but more reluctantly. Caesar demanded 200 hostages of Indutiomarus, including his son. He then proceeded to persuade the most important members of the tribe to support Cingetorix. Having settled this problem, Caesar marched to Portus Itius (probably Wissant). Here he assembled nearly 800 ships.

The wisdom of Caesar's going to Britain when Gaul was still far from securely under Roman control was questionable. Caesar himself realized that there was much dissatisfaction among the Gauls. To lessen the risk of removing himself and his legions from the area, he summoned the Gallic chieftains to the port, and told them that they would all have to go to Britain with him.

Leaving Labienus with three legions and 2,000 cavalry to

protect the ports, provide food supplies, and watch what was going on in Gaul, Caesar sailed just before sunset on an early July day. He had with him five legions and 2,000 cavalry. The Roman fleet was an impressive sight as it approached the coast of Britain the next afternoon. The army landed somewhere between Sandown and Sandwich. The display of power was enough to scare the Britons away from the beaches.

Caesar soon discovered a big concentration of the Britons about 12 miles away. Leaving his ships riding at anchor on an open shore he set off at midnight. Early in the morning the Roman cavalry repulsed a British cavalry and chariot attack, and the Britons withdrew to a stronghold in the forest. They were driven out, however, by the 7th Legion. Since it was late afternoon Caesar did not pursue, preferring first to entrench his camp. The next morning he sent light infantry and cavalry in pursuit but called them back after word came that nearly all of his ships had been wrecked or damaged or driven ashore in a great storm.

Returning in haste to the shore Caesar found that 40 of his ships were a total loss. The rest could be repaired. In accordance with the usual Roman practice the skilled artisans served also as legionaries and had to be called from soldiering to work on the ships. Caesar sent to Gaul for more workers and also ordered Labienus to put his men to work building ships. He had the surviving ships brought up on the beach and built a seawall to protect them.

The Britons took advantage of Caesar's preoccupation with his ships to combine forces under the command of Cassivellaunus, king of the Catuvellauni. Rather than attacking the

Roman camp, or risking a full-scale battle, the Britons embarked on a series of guerrilla actions. The Romans, trained for formal warfare, had difficulty in coping with these tactics.

Learning that the Britons were massed on the other side of the Thames River, Caesar marched his entire force to the site of the only ford in the area. The Britons were indeed drawn up for battle on the other side. They had, moreover, planted pointed stakes along the bank and in the mud of the river. Despite these obstacles Caesar sent his cavalry across the river. The legionaries followed quickly, easily evading the stakes. The combined attack drove the Britons away, with heavy losses.

Cassivellaunus disbanded most of his forces. With the remainder he followed the Roman army as it marched toward the land of the Trinovantes (modern Essex). He ordered all people and cattle that were in the Romans' path to seek refuge in the woods where he knew the invaders would not follow. Britons, hiding in these woods, harassed all Roman foraging parties which got too far from the main body. This kept the Romans to a narrow route, and prevented their destroying anything far from the line of march.

The Trinovantes made an alliance with Caesar and persuaded five other tribes to join them. They informed Caesar that he was not far from the stronghold of Cassivellaunus. (The Britons, said Caesar, called a "stronghold" any densely wooded spot fortified with a rampart and trench and used as a refuge against attack by marauding bands.) The Romans assaulted this crude fortification, drove out most of its occupants, and captured a great quantity of cattle.

This loss, and the failure of an attack which he had ordered

59

against the Roman naval camp, convinced Cassivellaunus that further resistance was useless. He asked for surrender terms. Caesar demanded hostages, and settled the amount of tribute that the Britons must pay annually to Rome. He forbade Cassivellaunus to bother the defecting Trinovantes.

Caesar then returned to the shore and departed for Gaul. He left no troops behind him, and it is doubtful if the tribute he had set was ever paid. He had in fact accomplished nothing of lasting importance to Rome. Furthermore, by absenting himself from Gaul that summer, he may have given the underlying unrest in Gaul a greater chance to grow.

The restlessness in Gaul was apparent to Caesar on his return, when he discovered that the grain crop had been poor. In an attempt to prevent trouble and to spread out the requisition of grain over a large area, he put all except one of the legions in Belgic territory for the winter, scattered in five separate camps. Caesar himself never left for Italy that winter, for before his legions were all settled in their camps, trouble had broken out.

CHAPTER 5

The First Gallic Rebellion Against Caesar

Rising of Ambiorix

Caesar had put his newest legion, recently enrolled and inexperienced, at Atuatuca, in the territory of the Eburones (probably near Liège). Throughout the territory of the Belgae, Indutiomarus, the deposed chief of the Treveri, had been stirring up anti-Roman sentiment ever since Caesar had supported Cingetorix against him. The presence of the Roman camps in the area seemed to him to offer an opportunity for action, and he persuaded the joint leaders of the Eburones—Ambiorix and Catuvolcus—to attack the camp at Atuatuca.

Ambiorix made an unsuccessful attempt to storm the camp, then from outside the walls called to the defenders to send out someone with whom he could talk. Two Roman officers came out, and to them Ambiorix professed his indebtedness to Caesar for having made him independent of the larger tribe of Atuatuci. He had attacked the Roman camp unwillingly, he said, because he could not refuse to participate in a plan supported by all the Gallic tribes to attack all the camps on that day. Then he urged the Romans to abandon the camp, for a large number of Germans were approaching to help the Gallic revolt. He would gladly provide an escort, he said, to the camp of Quintus Cicero, about 50 miles away, or to that of Labienus, a bit farther off.

The two Roman commanders, Sabinus and Cotta, called a council of war to consider the best move to make. Cotta was in favor of staying within the secure walls of the fortress. He was confident that they could hold out against Gauls and Germans alike. Sabinus was doubtful, however, and urged that they leave at once, before it was too late. He thought that Caesar must already have left for Italy and that they had better make their own decision to abandon their vulnerable position and seek the strength of another Roman camp. The centurions supported Cotta, but Sabinus was not a man to yield easily in an argument. At midnight Cotta finally agreed, and orders were issued to march at dawn.

The soldiers spent the rest of the night in preparation and were already tired when the long column emerged from the camp, trusting in the good faith of Ambiorix. Their trust was vain, however, for the chieftain and his men were lying in ambush. When the column and its baggage train had entered a ravine in the forest, the Eburones attacked it from front and rear. Only a few Romans survived the slaughter that followed and got away to report the disaster at the camp of Labienus.

Ambiorix immediately attempted to take advantage of his

victory. Riding as fast as he could, he stirred up the Atuatuci and the Nervii to join the Eburones. Together the three forces launched a heavy attack on the camp of Cicero, who had not yet heard of the loss of the other legion. Unable to take the camp by storm, the Gauls laid siege to it in the Roman fashion they had learned from Caesar. They encircled it with a wall and a trench, and built siege machinery with the help of Roman prisoners. Taking advantage of a strong wind, they threw red-hot darts over the walls and set fire to most of the buildings within. In a series of heavy fights at the ramparts many on both sides were killed. But the Romans repulsed every attack.

Some of the Nervian chiefs now asked Cicero for an interview. He met them just outside the gate, and they told him of what had happened to the other camp. Insisting that they were really faithful to Rome, they urged that he too withdraw his troops. Like Ambiorix, they promised to escort the Romans safely to another camp.

But Cicero refused to be taken in. He inspired his men to strengthen the fortifications and fight valiantly, until he could get help from Caesar. However, every messenger he tried to send was captured, then led in front of the camp to be tortured and killed in full view of the Roman defenders. Finally a Nervian defector was persuaded to send his slave in exchange for his freedom, and the slave succeeded in taking the word to Caesar, who was near Samarobriva (Amiens).

At once Caesar rounded up two understrength legions, about 7,000 men and 400 cavalry, and started to the rescue. He sent

63

orders to Labienus to join him. But Labienus was being threatened by the Treveri. He sent word that he could not leave his camp, and he also reported to Caesar on the fate of Sabinus.

Relief of Cicero

Caesar sent word ahead to Cicero by a Gallic horseman. Unable to enter the camp, the messenger tied the message to his spear and flung it over the wall at night. The spear was discovered by Cicero's men two days later, having stuck unnoticed in the woodwork of a tower. Soon afterward the defenders saw the smoke of burning villages in the distance and knew that help was at hand. The Gauls also learned that Caesar was approaching. They raised the siege and went to meet him. Cicero at once sent a message to Caesar that he was about to be intercepted. Caesar prepared to meet the Gauls on their own terms.

As soon as he sighted the Gauls, on the far side of a valley, Caesar halted and set his men to work building a fortified camp. He purposely made it small in order to make the Gauls think that he had fewer troops than he really had with him. When the Gallic horsemen raided across the valley to engage the Roman cavalry, Caesar ordered his men to fall back and to entice the Gauls to follow. He also had his soldiers put on a great show of confusion and panic within the camp as the Gauls approached.

The Gauls were completely fooled by these measures, and

were certain that they would have no trouble overwhelming Caesar. The whole Nervian force moved across the valley and prepared to storm the half-completed palisades. Suddenly Caesar gave a prearranged order. At a trumpet blast his troops rushed out from all four gates and attacked. At the same time the cavalry, which had pretended to flee, charged back when they heard the trumpet.

The surprised Gauls fled, leaving weapons and many casualties behind them. The survivors disappeared into the woods. Caesar called off the pursuit, then marched to Cicero's camp. He found less than a tenth of the men unwounded. After giving the wounded all possible assistance, Caesar prepared to go to the assistance of Labienus. But just as he was about to march, he learned this would not be necessary.

Labienus and Indutiomarus

Word of Caesar's victory near Cicero's camp had been sent speedily to Labienus, who was preparing to withstand an all-out assault by Indutiomarus and the Treveri. Indutiomarus also heard the news, however, and reconsidered. Instead of attacking Labienus, he withdrew, fearing the arrival of Caesar.

By this time Caesar had received reports that unrest was sweeping through Gaul. Only two groups of tribes, the Aedui and the Remi, could be trusted as remaining loyal to Rome. New reports of treachery and violence reached Caesar almost daily. He decided that the situation in Gaul was too unsettled for him to leave for Italy, and he decided to stay through the winter at Samarobriva.

During the winter Indutiomarus was also busy. He made contact with some of the German tribes, but these refused to join him. He was more successful, however, in building up support and obtaining men from all over Gaul. By midwinter, he felt strong enough to strike again.

Labienus' camp was on a naturally protected site, evidently on high, rocky ground. His men were well trained; and he received reliable information from Cingetorix, who told him what Indutiomarus was up to. So, when Indutiomarus reappeared, Labienus was alert and ready.

Indutiomarus set up a routine of patrols around the camp, trying to force the Romans to come out to fight. He planned to ambush them with his main body when they attacked the patrols. Labienus obtained some horsemen from the friendly tribes in the neighborhood, and secretly smuggled them into the camp at night. When a favorable opportunity appeared he sent the cavalry charging from both gates upon the unsuspecting Gauls, closely followed by the legionaries.

The Gauls, finding themselves unexpectedly attacked in their hiding places, fled in panic. The Roman soldiers hunted down Indutiomarus and returned triumphantly to camp, bearing the chieftain's head. All the other Gauls whom they could catch were slaughtered. The loss of Indutiomarus was a disaster to the rebellious Gauls, for he was at that time the only leader who might have unified them against the Romans.

The death of Indutiomarus by no means meant the end of trouble in Gaul, however, and Caesar was well aware that he might expect more uprisings. During the winter of his stay at Samarobriva he called up two new legions from Italy and persuaded Pompey to send him another from his command. These reinforcements more than made up for the troops lost with Sabinus.

Late in the winter of 54–53 B.C., Caesar decided to try to forestall a threatened outbreak by the Nervii, Atuatuci, and Menapii. He took four legions on a surprise raid into the land of the Nervii. Caught offguard, many of the Nervii were killed or captured, their large cattle herds were taken, and the countryside was devastated. The survivors soon surrendered.

In the early spring of 53 B.C., Caesar called the annual meeting of Gallic chieftains. Three of the tribes, the Senones, Carnutes, and Treveri, sent no representatives. Caesar interpreted this as a step toward armed rebellion and determined to stop it. He immediately ordered the meeting to be transferred to Lutetia (Paris), which was near the territory of the Senones. He set out at once for Lutetia with his legions.

Caesar's appearance in the area was enough. Acco, the Senone chief, submitted. The Aedui, who had been overlords of the Senones, supported his petition for pardon, and Caesar granted it. He took 300 hostages, however, which he turned over to the Aedui. When the Carnutes, backed by the Remi, made a similar appeal for mercy, he gave them the same terms. Central Gaul was thus pacified. After instructing the various loyal chieftains to send him cavalry, Caesar adjourned the meeting and turned his attention to Ambiorix and the Treveri, who were still rebellious.

Pacification of the North

Caesar's first move was to deprive Ambiorix of his allies, the Menapii, who lived in the coastal area of modern Belgium and the Netherlands. Alone among the Gallic tribes they had never offered to make terms with the Romans. Seven Roman legions descended on the land of the Menapii in three columns, building roads before them when necessary. They burned villages and destroyed crops as they went, seizing cattle and taking prisoners. The Menapii had no army with which to resist the Romans, and now they sued for peace. Caesar granted it, on condition that they not admit Ambiorix or his agents to their lands. Then he moved against the Treveri.

The Treveri had gathered a large army and were again marching to attack the camp of Labienus. Caesar had word of their plans, however, and quickly sent two legions to triple the force in the Roman camp. The Treveri halted when they learned of the arrival of the new legions and awaited some German reinforcements which were on the way.

Labienus took advantage of the situation to march out with two and one-half legions and some cavalry. He encamped across a river from the Treveri. Then, pretending to withdraw in haste and confusion he enticed the enemy across the river. Suddenly the Romans turned and attacked. The Treveri were completely surprised and fled, many being cut down or taken prisoner.

With the Treveri under control, Caesar continued his march to the Rhine with the purpose of discouraging the Germans from offering help to revolting tribes in Gaul or giving asylum to Ambiorix. He again built a bridge and crossed the Rhine into the territory of the friendly Ubii. He was planning to attack the Suebi, but they withdrew into the Thuringian Forest. With no supply of grain available, Caesar could not pursue them. He devastated some Suebi villages, then again he recrossed the river. He destroyed the eastern end of the bridge, but left twelve cohorts to defend the western end.

As fall approached, Caesar set out on the trail of Ambiorix, in the Eburone lands. He sent all his cavalry ahead under the command of Lucius Minucius Basilus. With the help of some friendly natives Basilus surprised Ambiorix, who had only a small group of cavalry with him. These nevertheless held off the Romans until Ambiorix could escape.

Caesar meanwhile had arrived at the old camp of Sabininus and Cotta. There he left all his heavy baggage and split up his force. Once again he garrisoned this camp, with his most inexperienced legion, the 14th, commanded by Quintus Cicero. He sent three legions under Labienus into the territory of the Menapii and another three under Trebonius to the land of the Atuatuci. He himself with the three remaining legions headed for the vicinity of Namur. All were to rejoin at the camp in a week, if the military situation permitted.

69

Ambiorix had ordered all rebellious Gauls in the region to look out for themselves, using guerrilla warfare. As Caesar's army marched through the forest, it was harassed by guerrillas. Caesar, preferring to sacrifice Gauls rather than Romans, sent out word to the neighboring tribes to join him in pillaging the territory of the Eburones. The response was great, and the whole area was soon being plundered by Gauls. Now it was the guerrillas who could not cope with the situation.

News of what was going on was carried across the Rhine, and 2,000 Sugambri horsemen made haste to accept Caesar's invitation to plunder. They rode through the area, gathering up herds of cattle and whatever they could lay hands on. They were thirsting for more as they approached the vicinity of the Roman camp at Atuatuca. Upon learning that all the Roman baggage was there and that Caesar was a long way off, they determined to seize this prize that seemed so readily available.

Cicero had been ordered by Caesar on no account to let anyone leave the camp before his return. His soldiers complained about this confinement, however. On the seventh day, when there was no sign of Caesar's return, Cicero sent out five cohorts, plus about 300 convalescent veterans, and a group of servants with pack animals, to reap the harvest in the fields nearby. Not long after they had left, the Sugambri dashed out of the woods and attacked the back gate of the camp. The troops inside panicked and Cicero barely managed to hold off the Sugambri as they tried again and again to break into the camp.

Suddenly the Sugambri spotted the troops sent out to harvest, who were by this time returning from the fields. The Germans ceased their efforts against the camp and attacked the small force from all sides. The inexperienced soldiers were terrified by this surprise barbarian onslaught. The convalescent veterans formed a wedge however; they broke through the enemy, and reached the camp in safety, followed by the servants and pack animals. Many of the others climbed a hill in an effort to get out of the way of the Sugambri, only to change their minds and try to dash across the lower ground to the camp. A few made it to safety, but most were surrounded and destroyed. Two entire cohorts were lost.

The Sugambri gave up the attempt to take the camp and rode off with their booty, back across the Rhine. The same evening Caesar's advance force of cavalry reached the scene, to find most members of the garrison still shaking with fear.

With the arrival of more horsemen from the Gallic tribes, the ravaging of the countryside continued. But although an enormous area was laid waste and every house and village was burned and all of the crops destroyed or consumed by men or animals, Ambiorix was never found. Time and again detachments came close to capturing him, but he always escaped.

By the beginning of winter Gaul was quiet. At last Caesar could return to Italy with confidence, leaving two legions among the Lingones (near Langres), two in the land of the Treveri, and six in the territory of the Senones. Before he left he had Acco, said to be the ringleader in the revolt of the Senones and the Carnutes, flogged to death "in the old Roman manner."

71

CHAPTER 6

The Rebellion of Vercingetorix

The Emergence of Vercingetorix

While Caesar was in Italy during the winter of 53–52 B.C., new unrest spread through Gaul. There was widespread resentment among the Gauls because of the severity of the measures he had taken to suppress the rebellion. Leaders of many of the Gallic tribes met secretly to plan a means of throwing off the Roman yoke. With Caesar away from his army, the Gallic leaders thought that a revolt would prevent him from rejoining. The Carnutes were given the task of lighting the fire of rebellion. The other tribal leaders swore solemnly that once the first blow was struck they would stick by the Carnutes until Gaul was free.

Roman tradesmen had settled in the chief town of the Carnutes, Cenabum (Orléans), as they had in most of the cities of Gaul by this time. They pursued their own business, and also assisted in supplying Caesar's army. One day late in 53 B.C., a band of Carnute tribesmen led by Cotuatus and Conconnetodumnus massacred all the Romans in Cenabum and seized their property. Within twelve hours word of the

72

massacre had been passed from mouth to mouth to reach 150 miles south, at the border of the land of the Arverni.

A young Arvernian prince named Vercingetorix, son of a former king, seized the opportunity to mobilize all of the Gauls in revolt. At first he was opposed by his uncle and some of the other Arverni chiefs, but he quickly gathered a powerful force, calling on them to fight in defense of liberty. Proclaimed king by his followers, Vercingetorix sent envoys to other tribes and soon had pledges of support from all over central and western Gaul. Before long he had assembled a large army, armed, organized, and very sternly disciplined, after the Roman manner. He sent a large force under the command of Lucterius, a Cadurcan, into the territory of the Ruteni, while he took the rest to the land of the Bituriges. Neither of these tribes had joined the revolt.

The Bituriges called on their overlords, the Aedui—allies of Rome—for help. Both Aeduan infantry and cavalry were sent in response to the appeal. But Vercingetorix's army was so strong that the Aeduans were afraid to cross the Liger River, which separated the Aeduan territory from the Bituriges. They gave up and returned home, whereupon the Bituriges joined Vercingetorix.

As soon as he heard what was going on, Caesar left Italy and set out for Transalpine Gaul. By the time he reached the Province he had discovered that all south-central Gaul was in revolt. He was confronted with the great problem of how to join his army, still in winter quarters in the north, hundreds of miles away. If he ordered his legions to join him, they would have to fight their

73

way through enemy-held territory without the benefit of his leadership. On the other hand, he did not dare trust any of the Gallic tribes to escort him safely to the winter camps of his army.

But there was a more immediate danger. Lucterius, having won over the Ruteni, was advancing on Narbo (Narbonne), in the Province itself. Caesar rushed to the city, reassured the frightened people there, and stationed detachments of the provincial garrison around the city. He stayed there to command the defense, but he ordered the rest of the garrison, and the bodyguard he had brought with him from Italy, to go to the land of the Helvii, close to the Arverni. The Helvii had not yet risen, and Caesar hoped this show of force would keep them loyal.

Lucterius did not dare attempt to break through the Roman guard to attack Narbo. When he withdrew, Caesar at once left to join his men among the Helvii. He had decided to fight his way through the land of the Arverni, and then on to rejoin his army in northern Gaul.

Caesar Regains the Initiative

It was midwinter, and a range of mountains, the Cévennes, lay between Caesar and his objective. The passes were blocked by snow, which completely concealed the road for miles. Nevertheless, Caesar's troops cut their way through and appeared on the borders of the territory of the astonished Arverni, who had considered the mountains impassable in winter. Caesar at once sent his cavalry across the border to harass the Arverni. The people pleaded with Vercingetorix to return to their defense.

When Vercingetorix approached, as Caesar had expected, Caesar turned over command of his troops to Decimus Brutus with instructions to keep on with the harassment of Arvernian territory, but to avoid battle. With a small escort, he himself took off at high speed for Vienne (Vienna), on the Rhone River. There he procured a fresh cavalry escort and sped on through the land of the Aedui to the territory of the Lingones, where two of his legions were wintering. He had sent word ahead summoning the rest of the legions. He assembled them all on the upper Matrona before word of what he was doing reached the Arverni.

Vercingetorix at once moved north and laid siege to the fortress of Gorgobina, where the Boii had been resettled after the defeat of the Helvetii. This was in central Gaul, west of the Liger, in the region between the Aedui and Bituriges.

Caesar decided that he must go to the aid of his allies, lest the few tribes that were still loyal should also desert him. He had to trust that the Aedui, on whom he was dependent for supply, would remain faithful. He marched due west, arriving after a day's march at Vellaunodunum in the land of the Senones. He took the town after a siege of three days. This gave him a base in the Sequana Valley to protect his supply line south to the Aedui. Two days later he was at Cenabum in Carnute territory. The inhabitants tried to flee from the city at night. But simultaneously Caesar sent in two legions in a night attack. They sacked the city and took most of the people prisoner.

Vercingetorix, hearing of Caesar's approach, dropped the siege of Gorgobina and hurried to meet him. The Romans were accepting the surrender of Noviodunum (Neuvy)—a town of the Bituriges—when the Gallic advance-guard cavalry appeared. Thanks to the staunchness of some 400 German cavalry that had been attached to the Roman army since the campaign against Ariovistus, the Gauls were driven off.

Scorched Earth

Vercingetorix at this point decided to change his strategy. Rather than attempt a direct confrontation with Caesar, he would attack the Roman supply lines, and prevent the Romans from living off the country. He called the Gallic chieftains together and got their approval of this policy. They reluctantly agreed to the drastic measure on which he insisted: to burn their homes and cities and to lay waste all the area through which the Roman army was likely to march. Against his better judgment, Vercingetorix agreed to an appeal from the Bituriges that Avaricum (Bourges), their largest and strongest town, should be spared. The Gauls sadly proceeded with the destruction of all other towns in central Gaul, burning as many as twenty in a single day.

Caesar meanwhile marched to the walls of Avaricum, fol-

76

lowed by Vercingetorix, who encamped about 15 miles away. Finding the city protected by a river and a marsh, Caesar moved into the small area of good ground where an approach was possible. At once he began to build siege towers and a ramp up to the city wall.

By this time, however the Roman food supply was running short, and the Gauls too were having difficulty finding fodder for their animals. Vercingetorix moved his camp closer to the city and sent parties out to attack the Roman foragers who went out daily looking for food.

The Gallic chief himself went off with some cavalry and light infantry to lay an ambush in an area where the foragers were expected to go the following day. But Caesar learned that Vercingetorix was away from his camp, and went out in the early morning to attack it. He found the Gauls formed up by tribes on a hill almost surrounded by a marsh. Caesar decided that it would be too dangerous to cross the marsh into the range of the waiting Gauls, and returned to camp.

Vercingetorix returned to find his men terrified of the Romans and on the verge of mutiny. He rallied them with a speech and then sent 10,000 picked troops into the city to assist in its defense.

The Gauls, said Caesar, were "a most ingenious race." They devised many ways of foiling Roman attempts to scale the walls and of destroying Roman siege machines. Finally Vercingetorix decided that the garrison should evacuate the city, under cover of night. The wives of the Gallic soldiers who were to leave, unable to dissuade their husbands from deserting them, made such a fuss that the Romans were warned of what was planned. Seeing that the Romans were alert, the Gauls gave up the plan and remained. The following day, in pouring rain, the Romans attacked and broke into the city. They spared no one. Of some 40,000 inhabitants only about 800 escaped.

At a conference of chieftains the following day, Vercingetorix expressed sorrow at what had happened, but blamed it on the mistaken desire of the Bituriges to save Avaricum. He promised victories in the future through a strong alliance, including tribes that had not yet joined him. And at once he set about acquiring more troops.

Caesar remained for several days in Avaricum, where there were large stores of grain and other provisions. Then he sent Labienus with four legions into the territory of the Senones and the Parisii to bring them into line. At the same time, Caesar himself took six legions down the east bank of the Elaver (Allier) River, toward Gergovia, the Arverni's chief town. Vercingetorix, upon hearing of this, ordered all bridges across the river destroyed and then followed Caesar on the opposite shore of the river.

With the Gauls camped across from them each night, the Romans were unable to build a bridge across the Elaver. So, before leaving camp one morning, Caesar hid two legions in a wooded area near a destroyed bridge. The rest of the army marched off, strung out to look as if the whole force were there. After waiting in hiding one day, the men who remained behind rebuilt the bridge, and the two legions crossed, to encamp on the other side, establishing a bridgehead. Caesar quickly marched back to cross the river. Word of this reached Vercingetorix, who hastened off, anxious to avoid an encounter with Caesar. Five days later the Romans were at Gergovia, 4 miles south of modern Clermont-Ferrand.

Siege of Gergovia

Gergovia was built on top of a small plateau, rising 1,200 feet from the plain, with steeply sloping sides that made it difficult to attack. South of it another steep hill, now known as the Roche Blanche, rose to a height some 500 feet lower than the main citadel. Vercingetorix installed his main force in camps on the slopes south and east of Gergovia, and also put a garrison on the Roche Blanche, for it overlooked the Auzon River and also protected access to the meadows along the river that were the chief source of forage.

Caesar at once decided that he could not take the city by direct assault and should besiege it. Having built a main camp southeast of Gergovia, he drove the Gallic detachment from the Roche Blanche in a night attack, and installed two legions there. From this position they could deprive the Gauls of their main source of water and limit the movement of their foragers. The two Roman camps were connected by two trenches, each about 6 feet wide, so that soldiers might pass freely from one to the

79

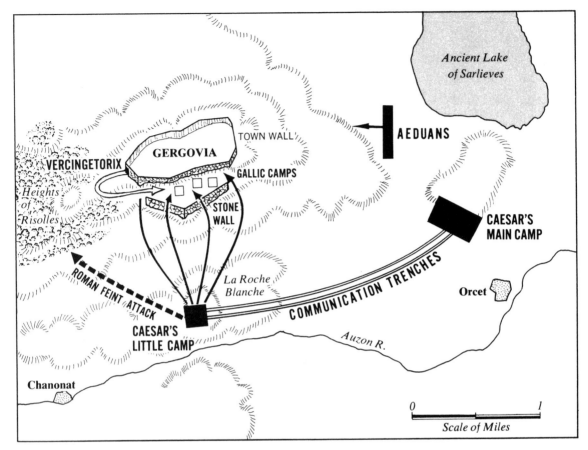

Siege of Gergovia.

other. Vercingetorix meanwhile strengthened the natural defenses of the hill where he was encamped with a 6-foot wall on its south slope.

Before Caesar could make any further moves, he had to cope with some serious unrest among the Aedui, who had been faithful to Rome for many years. While he was absent from the camp with four legions, Vercingetorix attacked it. Gaius Fabius, who had been left in command, held his post only with difficulty.

Soon after his return to camp, Caesar made a feint toward the wooded hills west of Gergovia. He sent packhorses disguised as cavalry and a whole legion in that direction. He secretly moved most of his remaining troops, probably four legions, to the smaller camp. Vercingetorix, not wishing the Romans to get on the hills overlooking his position, rushed the bulk of his forces to defend the high ground west of Gergovia. Caesar then ordered a direct assault on the Gallic camps on the slope of Gergovia, while some 10,000 Aeduan troops attacked from the right.

With little difficulty the Roman soldiers swarmed over the wall protecting the almost-deserted enemy camps and quickly captured three. Caesar, not wanting to risk his men in an uphill fight, tried to recall them, but only the 10th Legion heeded his summons. The others, either not hearing or not wishing to hear, rushed ahead and stormed the city wall itself. A few actually entered the town. At this point Vercingetorix rushed back with his men, attacked the Romans, who were rather disorganized by this time, and drove them out of the camps.

Caesar urgently ordered Titus Sextius, whom he had left with some cohorts in the small camp, to move out and take a position on the enemy's right flank southwest of Gergovia, to be prepared to cut off an enemy pursuit if necessary. Meanwhile, the Gauls had the advantage of numbers and of position as they fought fiercely with the Roman soldiers, driving them back down the hill. The 10th Legion checked the pursuing Gauls at

81

the foot of the hill, however. The Gauls then retired to their camps as the Romans sought refuge in theirs. Nearly 700 Roman soldiers, including 46 centurions, had perished.

Caesar reprimanded his troops the next day for their disobedience, while commending them for their courage. However, he said, "Men serving under me are expected to show obedience and self-restraint no less than high courage in the field." He then drew up his legions on the plain in line of battle on two successive days. This helped restore their confidence, for Vercingetorix declined to accept the offer of battle.

The Revolt Spreads

Caesar's situation was critical by this time. Although he had put down the Aeduan revolt he could no longer trust their loyalty. He now feared a full-scale uprising of all of the Gauls, and he decided that he must rejoin Labienus and the rest of the army before he was entirely encircled by hostile tribes. Breaking camp, he abandoned the siege and headed for the territory of the Aedui, again rebuilding a bridge in order to cross the Elaver. He wanted to get to his base in Aedui territory, Noviodunum.* There he kept his supplies, money, horses, and hostages.

As Caesar hastened north, some of the Aeduans revolted and massacred the Roman garrison at Noviodunum. They distrib-

* There were apparently several Noviodunums in Gaul, one was in the land of Bituriges, and another in Aedui territory.

uted the money and horses and some of the grain, and burned down the city. Then they raised troops from the tribe and stationed them along the Liger River, which Caesar must cross on his way north. He fooled them, however, by moving so fast that he reached the river and crossed it by a ford before the Aedui expected him. He then proceeded northeastward into the land of the Senones.

Meanwhile Labienus had left his base at Agedincum (Sens) and despite opposition had gone to Lutetia, which was burned by the Gauls just before he got there. At almost the same time he heard that the Bellovaci were preparing to join the revolt and also heard a false rumor that Caesar, having failed to cross the Liger, was returning to the Province. Labienus marched back to Agedincum to pick up his baggage train. Then he headed south to join Caesar if possible. He had to fight a stubborn battle with a large and well-equipped Gallic army led by Camulogenus, but Labienus was successful. Three days later he joined Caesar, who had been marching to meet him.

With the defection of the Aedui the revolt embraced almost all the Gallic tribes. At a council at Bibracte, attended by representatives of the tribes, Vercingetorix was confirmed as overall leader of the Gauls. In an attempt to win over the Allobroges in the upper Rhone Valley, he sent a force of 10,000 infantry and 800 cavalry into their territory. Other tribes were ordered to invade the Roman Province, and to try to obtain the support of the Helvii in the central Rhone Valley, and of the Volcae Arecomici, near the Mediterranean coast.

The Helvii were defeated by the invading Arverni, but

83

Caesar frustrated the other plans by ordering Lucius Caesar, who was serving as his deputy in the Province, to raise twenty-two new cohorts and station them around the Province. The Allobroges remained faithful and strongly fortified the banks of the Rhone River.

Caesar, aware that his cavalry was much weaker than that of Vercingetorix, sent to friendly German tribes for more horsemen. Then, with his army concentrated, he started south for the Province, by a route that would take him through the territory of the Lingones into the land of the Sequani, as he headed for the valley of the Arar River. Because of the extent of the revolt he apparently had decided to abandon most of his conquests in central Gaul, and to start over again from his main base in the Province.

Vercingetorix went out to meet the Romans, setting up camps on the Vingeanne, near modern Dijon. The following day he divided his cavalry in three groups. He sent two of these to harass the Roman column as it advanced along the road, and one to block its path in an ambush. It appears that Caesar was surprised by the attack, but he and his troops were alert. He formed his infantry in a hollow square with the baggage on the inside, while his cavalry fought off the Gallic horsemen. Finally Caesar's German cavalry was able to secure a hill, driving off the Gauls who had been defending it. The rest of the Gallic horsemen broke and fled.

With his cavalry defeated, Vercingetorix withdrew westward with his infantry to the stronghold of Alesia, in the land of the Mandubii. Caesar at once sensed that this minor cavalry defeat had discouraged the Gauls out of all proportion to the scale of

Alesia from the northeast.

the engagement. He abandoned his plan to retreat to the Province, and vigorously pursued Vercingetorix to Alesia.

The Investment of Alesia

Alesia stood on a flat-topped hill now known as Mont Auxois, not far from modern Dijon. About 500 feet high, 1¼ miles long, and ½ mile wide, the hill lies between the Ose and Oserain rivers. On three sides the plateau is surrounded by hills of about the same height, but on the west a plain extends between the streams as they flow toward the Brenne River. The sloping sides of the plateau formed a natural defense for the city, whose walls were built along the edges of the flat top.

The day after the cavalry engagement, Caesar arrived near Alesia, to find Vercingetorix and the Gauls encamped on the eastern slope, outside the city walls. To strengthen their position

85

they were completing a ditch and a 6-foot wall in front of them, between the two rivers. They apparently expected the attack to be made from that side.

After inspecting the area, Caesar decided against trying a direct attack, recalling the problems of an uphill assault at Gergovia. Instead he would blockade the city and the Gallic army. He established eight camps at strategic points around the city, putting infantry on the hilltops and cavalry near the streams. He planned to link these camps with 9½ miles of trenches and earthen walls, studded with twenty-three redoubts. Guards were posted day and night.

Shortly after the work began, Vercingetorix sent his cavalry out on the plain to challenge the Romans. At first Caesar's horsemen had a hard time. But when he sent in the German cavalry and drew up the legions in impressive array outside their camps, the tide changed. The Germans pushed ahead and drove the Gauls in disorder back to their camp, killing many as they fled.

Vercingetorix then made a decision that greatly weakened his position. That night he sent his cavalry away, with orders to return to their respective tribes and to muster all men of military age to come to his relief. He had, he said, supplies for thirty days for his 65,000 remaining men. Forage for the 10,000–15,000 horsemen was undoubtedly more than Vercingetorix could have provided, but by depriving himself of all his cavalry he greatly limited his operational capabilities. At the least they could have seriously hindered Caesar's vital foraging parties.

Once the cavalry had gone, Vercingetorix moved all his

troops inside the city walls, into an area which must have been crowded indeed. He distributed all the cattle between the garrison and the people, and set up a central grain supply, which he doled out in small quantities in order to make it last as long as possible.

Caesar's Siege Lines

Caesar was unable to intercept the departing Gallic horsemen. He realized that other Gauls would soon be massing forces to come to the relief of beleaguered Alesia. He had three main problems: how to keep Vercingetorix in; how to prevent a relief army from breaking through; and how at the same time to feed his own large army, at least 50,000 strong. To meet the problems he first strengthened his defenses.

The complicated barriers that Caesar constructed to protect his army, and to keep the Gauls outside from reaching the Gauls inside, are described in detail in Caesar's own book, *Commentaries on the Gallic Wars*. Recent archeological excavations in the area have established the accuracy of his description.

At the foot of the western slope of the plateau the soldiers dug a deep ditch 20 feet wide to prevent the Gauls in the stronghold from getting to the plain. About 400 feet west of this, the Romans constructed a wall 12 feet high facing the city; from the parapet, stakes projected outward and downward to hinder scalers from the city side. Towers were built at 130-

yard spaces along the wall. This wall was continued to encircle the city except where slopes were too steep or rock was too near the surface to permit digging. The wall connected the various camps and strongholds already built, extending about 11 miles.

To strengthen the position further and reduce the number of men required to hold the line, in front of the wall there was an ingenious system of obstacles, most of them invented by Caesar or his men. Two parallel trenches were built, the one nearer the wall in such a way that water from the Oserain River could be diverted into it. In long trenches 5 feet deep, five rows of thick branches, with bark and leaves removed and having sharpened ends, were planted close together. In front of these was a series of conical pits 3 feet deep. In each of these a log several inches thick was stuck end down, with a fire-sharpened point at the upper end protruding 3 inches above the ground. These were covered with twigs and branches to make them less visible. The Roman soldiers called them "lilies," because they resembled those flowers. In front of them the Romans set a number of 2-foot logs with iron hooks projecting outward.

To protect the army from attack from outside the city, a second line of fortifications was built some distance from the first, facing the other way. The line of circumvallation* was 13 miles long.

Vercingetorix sent out troops constantly to harass the Roman soldiers as they worked. But in spite of this the defenses were

* A line of contravallation is built to defend besiegers against sorties from an invested fortress. A line of circumvallation is built to defend besiegers from a relief army.

completed in about forty days. This was a tremendous accomplishment, a tribute to the men, to their devotion to their leader, and to the Romans' engineering skill. During this period, too Roman foraging parties roamed far from the base, gathering enough to provide each man with an emergency supply of food for thirty days.

Arrival of the Gallic Rebel Army

Meanwhile, Vercingetorix's horsemen had ridden through Gaul, delivering his message. The chieftains met and agreed that each tribe should furnish a certain number of men for an army. Rapidly the men assembled, probably in the land of the Aedui. Only the Bellovaci did not fill their quota, asserting that they preferred to fight alone. With confidence this vast army started for Alesia, some 250,000 infantry and 9,000 horsemen, with four men in joint command: Commius, whom Caesar had not long before made king of the Atrebates; two Aeduans—Viridomarus and Eporedorix; and a son-in-law of Vercingetorix, Vercassivellaunus.

Vercingetorix meanwhile was losing hope of rescue, for it took longer than he anticipated to assemble this relief force. Before it reached Alesia supplies within the city ran out. In desperation the Gauls considered eating the oldest and youngest people, who could not fight. Instead they drove the Mandubii, the civilian inhabitants, out of the city. As this large group ap-

89

proached the Roman walls that barred them from leaving the area, they begged to be taken in and fed, even as slaves. But Caesar refused to receive them. He knew that if he let them through, it would help the defenders. His account gives no hint of their ultimate fate.

At about this time the Gallic relieving army arrived nearby, and camped on a hill (Mussy-la-Fosse) west of the Roman circumvallation. The next day the Gallic cavalry rode onto the plain, almost entirely filling it. The besieged in Alesia were so cheered at this sight that they came outside the city walls and some rushed to fill in the 20-foot ditch. Caesar mustered his men on both walls and sent out his cavalry to meet the Gallic challenge. The fight lasted all afternoon, until Caesar's German horsemen, swooping down in a mass attack, finally drove the Gauls from the field, killing most of the archers that had accompanied them, and totally disheartening Vercingetorix's men.

The relief army spent the next day preparing crude siege machinery: grappling hooks, scaling ladders, and branches to fill in the ditches. At midnight they approached the Roman defenses and started filling in the trenches. As soon as the noise reached the troops in Alesia, they too came out and in turn tried to approach from their side. Roman soldiers, firing stones and stakes from catapults and ballistae on the walls, hit many of the attackers even in the darkness, while the various devices and obstacles outside the walls took their toll. As day broke, the Gauls on the outside, fearing a flank attack from the Roman camps on either side, withdrew. Once more Vercingetorix and his men retired into the city.

The Final Battle for Alesia

North of Alesia, Caesar had been forced to build a camp on the lower slope of a hill (Mont Rea) that was too large to encircle with the defense walls. There he had stationed two legions. The Gauls, reconnoitering the area, discovered this camp and soon realized that it was vulnerable to an attack from the hill. Under cover of night Vercassivellaunus moved to the area with 60,000 men. The following day, at noon, his men attacked, while at the same time Gallic cavalry approached the wall where it faced the plain. The rest of the Gallic infantry paraded in front of their camps but took no part in the action. Vercingetorix, on the other side, moved in force to attack the Roman defenses opposite the threatened camp.

Fighting was desperate in all three areas. Caesar, stationed on a height where he could watch the whole battlefield, moved forces repeatedly to areas that were particularly hard pressed. At the camp, the Gauls filled in the obstacles. Climbing on hastily built dirt ramps, or on massed men holding shields over their backs in the formation known as a *testudo*, many reached the top of the wall and some entered the camp. As the camp defenders tired and their ammunition ran low, Caesar sent Labienus with six cohorts with orders to hold the camp as long as possible, but if necessary to fight his way out. Caesar himself visited the areas where action was heaviest and by his presence cheered the men and inspired them to keep up the fight.

Vercingetorix, who had been making little headway against the wall on the west, shifted his men and his apparatus and

91

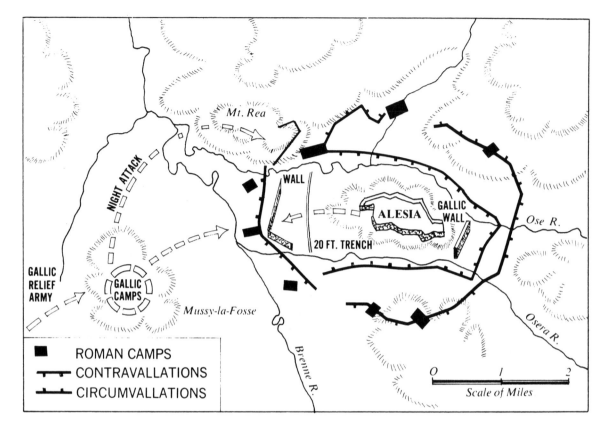

Siege of Alesia.

assaulted the wall where it crossed a hill south of the city. There he did better, and his attack was so successful that Caesar sent two sizable reinforcements to the area, and finally went himself with a fresh detachment. This turned the tide, and the Gauls were driven back toward the city.

By this time the situation in the camp was desperate. Taking five fresh cohorts and some cavalry, Caesar headed there, sending a separate detachment of cavalry around outside the walls to attack the rear of Vercassivellaunus' force. As Caesar came marching down the hill, wearing his bright scarlet cloak over his armor, the enemy, as well as his own men, recognized him.

From all sides a great shout arose. The hard-pressed legionaries fell to with their swords as new men came up to help them. They were already gaining the upper hand when suddenly Caesar's horsemen charged into the Gallic rear. The Gauls broke and fled, many of them to be cut down by the cavalry, which mercilessly continued the pursuit for miles. The rest of the Gallic army, watching the action from their camps on the hill, made no move to support their allies.

Surrender of Vercingetorix

Vercingetorix, seeing what had happened, abandoned hope and withdrew into the city. After a meeting of the Gallic chiefs in the city, Alesia surrendered next day to Caesar. Vercingetorix himself, "the chief spring of all the war," says Plutarch, "putting his best armor on, and adorning his horse, rode out of the gates, and made a turn about Caesar as he was sitting, then quitting his horse, threw off his armor, and remained quietly sitting at Caesar's feet until he was led away to be reserved for the triumph."

The triumph was to be delayed for six years. Afterward Vercingetorix was put to death, a sorry end for a mighty warrior and a worthy opponent of Julius Caesar. Had he continued his policy of trying to keep Caesar from supplies, and avoided a

93

direct confrontation, the outcome in Gaul might have been very different.

Caesar separated the Aedui and the Arverni from the rest of the prisoners, whom he distributed among his men. The troops then sold these prisoners as slaves to the traders who always accompanied the Roman armies. Caesar took the Aedui and Arverni prisoners back to the land of the Aedui, where they were repatriated. In return both tribes swore allegiance to Rome and gave Caesar numerous hostages. With these two powerful peoples on his side again, Caesar felt that Gaul was reasonably secure. He then distributed his legions in winter quarters scattered through the whole region and himself spent the winter of 52–51 B.C. at Bibracte. When word of the great victory at Alesia reached Rome, twenty days of public thanksgiving were decreed.

Final Pacification of Gaul

Although nothing like a united effort to overthrow Roman control in Gaul occurred again after the surrender of Alesia, various Gallic tribes continued to give trouble. In December, 52 B.C., Caesar led two legions to put down unrest among the Bituriges.

Hardly had he returned to Bibracte than the Bituriges called on him to help them put a stop to raids by the Carnutes. Caesar proceeded to Cenabum with two legions. While the bulk of his forces encamped, his cavalry drove off the raiders, and helped by very cold weather, killed or dispersed them.

Meanwhile the Bellovaci, led by their chief, Correus, were mustering an army to attack the Suessiones. The Remi, overlords of the Suessiones, sent word of this threat to Caesar. Taking four legions, he marched into the land of the Bellovaci, where he learned that Correus, with his tribe and other allies, was encamped on a hill (Mt. St. Marc) in the forest of Compiègne, protected by a marsh. Some prisoners told Caesar that Correus intended to fight Caesar if he had three legions or less with him, but otherwise would only attack Roman foragers.

On the strength of this information, Caesar formed his men in three columns so that they would appear to be three legions, and moved up to occupy a hill (Mt. St. Pierre) which faces St. Marc across a deep ravine. There was some skirmishing between the two forces, and Caesar decided he would have to lay siege to the enemy camp, since it was too well protected to be stormed. So he sent for Trebonius to come with three legions as fast as possible.

The Bellovaci, on hearing rumors of Caesar's intention, decided to evacuate their camp. One night they started sending all their noncombatants and their baggage train out of the camp, with the intention of following soon after with fighting men. But only part of the baggage had gone when daylight revealed the situation to the Romans. Rapidly Caesar built a bridge of logs across the marsh and moved his army to occupy a ridge that led almost to the Bellovaci camp. There they waited.

The Bellovaci formed in battle line while the rest of the noncombatant elements withdrew. In front of their line they piled heaps of straw and sticks. As darkness fell, at a given signal the Bellovaci applied the torch all along the line. Suddenly a wall of flame concealed them from the Romans, and the Gallic troops turned and ran. Caesar tried to in vain to get his cavalry through the thick smoke. Unpursued, the Bellovaci escaped to a camp on the Isara (Oise) River, about 9 miles away. From there they attacked Roman foraging parties who ventured near.

Finally Caesar learned that Correus had a plan to ambush Roman foragers, hiding 6,000 infantrymen and 1,000 horsemen in the woods near a plain where the foragers often went. Caesar accordingly sent out his foragers with cavalry and lightly armed infantrymen as escorts and followed at a distance with a body of heavy infantry. When Correus emerged from the woods, Caesar attacked. Half the Bellovaci were killed; the rest fled.

Caesar then moved on to the Bellovaci camp. Some of the chieftains fled as Caesar came up; the rest surrendered. When Caesar treated the Bellovaci leniently, as he had the Bituriges, most of the other rebellious states also submitted to him.

There was one important exception to Caesar's new policy of leniency. Ambiorix, who had given him so much trouble a few years before, apparently was stirring up trouble again. Although he fled, Caesar went into the territory of Ambiorix's people, the Eburones, and devastated it with fire and sword. A large part of the population was killed or taken prisoner, as Caesar vented his anger at Ambiorix on the land and the people.

There was one more incident which required Caesar's attention before the rebellion in Gaul was finally put down. Caius Caninius and Caius Fabius severely defeated a chief of the Andes, Dumnacus, who had laid siege to Limonum (Poitiers), in the land of the Pictones. But some 2,000 fugitives, led by chiefs named Drappes, a Senonian, and Lucterius, of the Cadurci, banded together and marched south toward the Province. With Caninius in close pursuit the Gauls realized they could not hope for success, and they took refuge on the hill of Uxellodunum (Puy d'Issolu), near the Duranius (Dordogne) River. So steep and rocky was this hill that further fortifications were unnecessary.

Caninius realized that it was impossible to storm the hill. At once he put his two legions to work building a line of contravallation in order to besiege the mountain fortress. The two Gallic chiefs, determined not to suffer the fate of Alesia, left the camp and headed a large band of foragers, who collected great quantities of grain in a camp 10 miles from Uxellodunum. Each night Lucterius led supply trains up into the fortress. Finally this procedure was discovered by the Romans and one of the supply trains was ambushed. Lucterius escaped, but from some of the prisoners Caninius learned where the supply camp was and surprised it, capturing Drappes.

Caesar meanwhile had gone to Cenabum and demanded the surrender of Cotuatus, who had started the whole revolt by the massacre of the Romans in that city. After Cotuatus had been flogged and beheaded, Caesar proceeded to Uxellodunum with

97

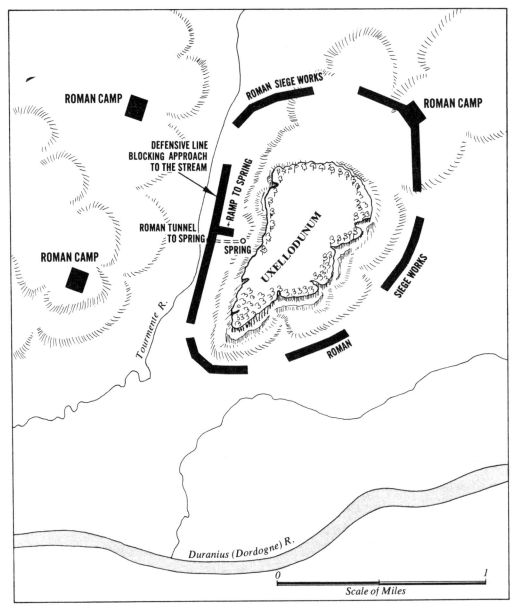

ROMAN CAMP

ROMAN SIEGE WORKS

ROMAN CAMP

DEFENSIVE LINE
BLOCKING APPROACH
TO THE STREAM

RAMP TO SPRING

ROMAN TUNNEL
TO SPRING

SPRING

UXELLODUNUM

ROMAN CAMP

SIEGE WORKS

ROMAN

Tourmente R.

Duranius (Dordogne) R.

0   1

Scale of Miles

Siege of Uxellodunum.

Ramp and tower at Uxellodunum.

his cavalry, followed by the legionaries. Fabius, having received submission of the Carnutes and other tribes in northwestern Gaul, had also joined Caninius by this time.

Caesar at once decided that the only way to take Uxellodunum was to cut off its water supply. He blocked the approaches to the stream that flowed below the fortress with archers, slingers, and catapults. But a spring close under the western end of the hill presented a greater problem. Using large wooden shields to protect the workers, Caesar had a great ramp built up toward the spring, and a ten-story tower constructed on top of it. At the same time a tunnel was started toward the spring to divert its water.

The besieged in Uxellodunum constantly attacked the workers and finally rolled barrels down the hill, filled with burning pitch which set fire to the Roman works. At the same time the Gauls attacked fiercely, inflicting considerable losses on the Romans. When Caesar sent a number of groups to pretend attacks at various points around the hill, the Gauls withdrew to protect their defenses and the Romans extinguished the fires. In time the tunnel reached the spring and the water was diverted.

Overcome by thirst, and convinced that the drying up of the spring was an act of the gods, the defenders of Uxellodunum surrendered. Caesar decided to make the incident an example for all Gaul. He spared the lives of the warriors, but he had the hands of all who had borne arms cut off. Drappes starved himself to death in captivity. Lucterius fled from one place to another until he was finally betrayed and delivered to Caesar.

This completed the conquest of Gaul. There were minor incidents thereafter but none on a scale that required Caesar himself to handle them.

Caesar spent the rest of the summer visiting the tribes of Aquitania. When the legions went into winter quarters he traveled to the Province to take care of administrative matters. Then he went north and spent the winter of 51–50 B.C. at Nemotocenna (Arras), among the Belgae.

Caesar's last year in Gaul, 50 B.C., was peaceful. He strengthened relations with the Gallic tribes, confirming their allegiance. After a grand review of all his troops in the land of the Treveri, he returned to Ravenna, in order to be near Rome when his command expired at the end of the year.

CHAPTER 7

The Rubicon and Spain

Turmoil in Rome

During the years that Caesar spent in Gaul, political unrest had increased in Rome. Rioting had become common, rival elements clashed in street fights, or used force to carry their measures in the Assembly. The loose bonds that had held the Triumvirate—Caesar, Crassus, and Pompey—together had rapidly disintegrated. Increasingly supporters of Pompey and of Caesar vied with each other in an obvious contest for the supreme power in Rome.

In 56 B.C. the three men had met at Luca in Cisalpine Gaul and agreed that Pompey and Crassus should hold consulships in the following year, that thereafter Pompey was to be proconsul in Spain while Crassus went to Syria. Both proconsulship terms were to be for five years, and Caesar's governorship in Transalpine Gaul, Cisalpine Gaul, and Illyricum would be extended for five years more.

On completion of his term as consul, Pompey sent others to govern his Spanish provinces for him, and himself stayed in Italy to superintend the supply of grain and to recruit troops.

101

Supposedly this was for his army in Spain but actually he was strengthening his position in Italy. In November, 54 B.C., Crassus went to Syria. The following year he was killed in a battle with the Parthians at Carrhae, in the worst defeat suffered by Rome since the Battle of Cannae. This left Caesar and Pompey with only each other as possible rivals for the first place in Rome.

In 53 B.C. the consular elections were repeatedly postponed by bribery and violence. Finally, on January 18, 52 B.C., Caesar's man Clodius was killed in a street fight with one of his political opponents. His body was dragged to the Senate House and set afire. The building burned down, as did several others nearby. Chaos reigned in the city until the Senate appointed Pompey sole consul and gave him power to raise an army and restore order in the city.

Caesar, meanwhile, realized that his governorship was about to come to an end, and with it the command of his army and the special privileges of his office. He did not wish to risk a period in which he would be out of power. This would present his political enemies with an opportunity to prosecute him for various things he had done during his first consulship, or by other means deprive him of the chance to regain power. His plan was to become consul for a second time on his return to Rome. To assure attaining that office he decided to arrange to keep command of his army until he became consul. Pompey, well recognizing Caesar's intentions, decided to oppose this plan, because he knew that he would have no trouble retaining supreme power in Rome if he could keep his army, while Caesar had none.

Since Pompey did not want an open break with Caesar, he complied with Caesar's request to secure passage of a law to enable him to stand for the consulship in absentia. Pompey also extended his own proconsulship in Spain, with the army that went with it. But he took no action on Caesar's request for an extension of his proconsulships of Cisalpine Gaul, Transalpine Gaul, and Illyricum.

Agitation was growing among Caesar's enemies in Rome for his relief from command in Gaul before the expiration of his term as governor. For the year 50 B.C. two of these foes, Lucius Aemilius Paullus and Gaius Claudius Marcellus, were elected consuls. Another supporter of Pompey and strong opponent of Caesar, Gaius Scribonius Curio, was elected tribune. Caesar, in preparation for the showdown he knew was coming, put some of the wealth he had acquired in Gaul to good use in his own cause to bribe Aemilius Paullus and Curio to shift sides to support him.

When Marcellus tried to appoint successors for Caesar in his governorships, Curio proposed that if Caesar must lay down his command Pompey must do so also. Pompey agreed to this on the condition that Caesar relinquish his command first. Curio then vetoed the whole thing, and the year passed without action.

As a result of the disaster to Crassus' army, the Senate voted that Caesar and Pompey should each send a legion to help protect Syria from possible Parthian attack. Pompey promptly agreed to send the one he had lent Caesar for operations in Gaul several years earlier. Thus Caesar had to send two legions to Rome. But first he paid the men well to ensure their loyalty to him. He also instructed the leaders to spread a false rumor that

103

the remainder of Caesar's army was in poor shape and would defect to Pompey as soon as it returned to Italy. The two legions never went to Syria, but were stationed instead in Capua by Pompey.

In December, 50 B.C., Caesar went to Ravenna, just north of the border of Roman Italy and Cisalpine Gaul. Affairs soon moved to a climax. On December 1, Marcellus had secured passage by the Senate of a directive to send successors to take over from Caesar, while a decree was issued that Pompey should not be deprived of his command. Curio then moved that, in order to avoid the civil war which everyone dreaded, both men should relinquish their commands. This measure was passed by an overwhelming vote, but was vetoed by a tribune loyal to Pompey. Then Marcellus went to Pompey and asked him to lead the two legions from Capua against Caesar, raising more troops as needed. Pompey accepted the commission but waited to see what was going to happen. Neither he nor Caesar wanted to be blamed for starting a civil war.

Curio rushed to Ravenna to tell Caesar of this situation. He urged Caesar to bring up his whole army and march on Rome. But instead Caesar, knowing the proposal would be unacceptable to Pompey, sent word that if he might retain two legions and the governorship of Cisalpine Gaul and Illyricum, he would give up Transalpine Gaul and the legions stationed there. Pompey pretended to agree, but the consuls turned it down. Thereupon Caesar sent Curio back to Rome with an ultimatum. He listed all that he had done in his career, then proposed "that he would lay down his command at the same time as Pompey, but

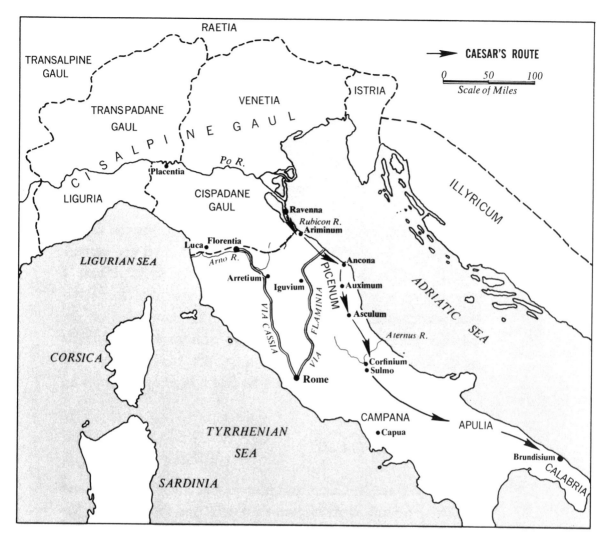

Italy in 50 B. C.

that if Pompey should retain his command he would not lay down his own, but would come quickly and avenge his country's wrongs and his own."

On January 1, 49 B.C., when Curio delivered the letter, it

105

was to new consuls who had taken office that day, Lucius Cornelius Lentulus and Gaius Claudius Marcellus (evidently a cousin of the previous consul of the same name). The following day the Senate voted that Caesar must disband his army by March 1 or be considered a traitor. At once the resolution was vetoed by Mark Antony and Quintus Cassius, tribunes supporting Caesar.

On January 3 and 4 the Senate did not meet, but the debate was resumed on the fifth. It was so heated that on the seventh Antony and Cassius were warned to leave the Senate House if they wished to avoid violence. On their departure the resolution was passed. This was illegal, and the expulsion of the tribunes gave Caesar a basis for his argument that popular rights were being trampled on, since the tribunes were the political voice of the people. Now he had a legal reason for war.

"The Die Is Cast"

Antony, Cassius, Curio, and Marcus Caelius Rufus, disguised as slaves, rushed to Ariminum (Rimini), the last town in Roman Italy, just across the border from Ravenna. The news of what had happened in Rome reached Caesar before the day was ended. He at once paraded his troops of the 13th Legion. He told the soldiers that they had been called public enemies and that Antony and Cassius had been illegally driven from the city.

Although Caesar had already sent for two more legions to

join him, he decided not to wait, but to proceed into Italy with the 5,000 infantry and 300 cavalry of the 13th Legion. On January 10 he sent a picked body of soldiers to occupy Ariminum. Late in the day he set off by carriage, escorted by his cavalry. When he reached the Rubicon (Fiumicino) River, which marked the boundary between Cisalpine Gaul and Roman Italy, he paused. According to Appian he said to those around him, "My friends, stopping here will be the beginning of sorrow for me; crossing over will be such for all mankind." He had made his choice. "The die is cast!" he said, and crossed the bridge over the Rubicon to civil war.

When he thus challenged the Roman Senate, Caesar had available to him eight legions in Gaul in addition to the 13th which he was leading. Two of these, the 8th and the 12th, were on their way to join him.

Caesar was well aware of the task before him. He could not hope to fight in Italy as he had in Gaul. He was prepared to fight, but more importantly he must win the support of the population, for he could not hope to impose his will permanently as a conqueror. Hence the harsh methods he had often used in Gaul—knowledge of which struck fear into the hearts of many Romans as he approached—were replaced by kindness, generosity, and persuasion.

Pompey apparently was at first not sure of the best course to take. He had little faith in the loyalty of the legions that had come from Gaul to Capua. He had three legions in Italy—the two at Capua and a third of recent recruits—and seven in Spain. He had other troops scattered in the provinces of

Syria, Asia, and Africa. Pompey also commanded all the warships of the Roman fleet. Yet he had last led an army in battle in 62 B.C., and none of his troops had the personal loyalty to him that Caesar's did to their general.

Pompey, controlled by the Senate, did not even have absolute power over his army. He was reluctant to risk a direct confrontation before he could develop an army whose loyalty to him was unquestioned. Hence he decided to abandon Rome and go to Macedonia. Caesar might take Italy, but Pompey intended to rally the legions in Spain and the forces in the East and return in triumph, closing in on Caesar from both sides.

The Senate sent envoys to Caesar on January 17, informing him that Lucius Domitius Ahenobarbus had been appointed to replace him in Gaul. At the same time Pompey sent a private letter urging Caesar not to injure the state. In response, Caesar proposed that all armies be disbanded and suggested that Pompey come to confer with him in an effort to settle the dispute. But he suspected that Pompey was merely trying to gain time, and did not await an answer.

Caesar Marches South

Caesar advanced south from Ariminum to Ancona, occupying the main towns on the way. He sent Antony with a detachment to take Arretium (Arezzo), on the Via Cassia, while Curio occupied Iguvium (Gubbio), on the Via Flaminia. Thus Caesar controlled the two main roads to Rome.

On the same day that the envoys reached Caesar, Pompey ordered the Senate and the consuls to leave Rome with him for Capua. There he received Caesar's reply. Pompey responded at once. He refused to meet Caesar, but he agreed to the suggestion that the armies be disbanded, on the condition that Caesar first withdraw his troops from the Italian towns which he had occupied. These terms were, of course, unsatisfactory to Caesar, and he rejected them. He resumed his southern advance to Auximum (Osimo) in the province of Picenum. The people welcomed him, and many of the defending garrisons defected to Caesar's army.

Caesar marched toward Asculum (Ascoli), which was defended by ten cohorts under Lentulus Spinther. As he approached, most of the troops deserted to him, and the rest fell back with Lentulus toward Corfinium (Pentima), where Domitius Ahenobarbus had twenty cohorts of new recruits. At about this time Caesar was joined by the 12th Legion. Continuing rapidly southward, he secured a bridge over the Aternus (Pescara) River before troops sent out by Domitius could demolish it. Caesar marched on to encamp outside the walls of Corfinium on February 15.

Domitius, as the newly appointed proconsul for Gaul, was not under Pompey's command. But Pompey had urged that they join forces at Capua. While Domitius was thinking about this, not sure whether he should stay at Corfinium, Caesar surprised him by appearing outside the walls. Domitius at once sent urgently to Pompey for assistance. Pompey, in turn, begged Domitius to join him in Apulia as soon as possible, for division of their forces meant weakness. He did not trust his own legions to remain loyal if he should take them to Corfinium, close to Caesar.

Caesar meanwhile had picked up seven cohorts that Domitius had left as a garrison at Sulmo (Sulmona). On February 17 the 8th Legion arrived from the north, enabling Caesar to surround Corfinium. At daybreak on the twenty-first the garrison surrendered. Caesar restrained his men from plundering, and he released Domitius, Lentulus, and the numerous other noblemen and high officials who were in the town. The soldiers were forced to take an oath of allegiance to Caesar. This brought Caesar's strength to six legions, about 30,000 men.

As soon as these matters were settled, Caesar struck his camps and set out by forced marches for Apulia. He suspected that Pompey was making for Brundisium, to take ship for Macedonia. Caesar was anxious to get to Brundisium first and force Pompey to fight.

When Caesar reached Brundisium, on March 9, he found that the consuls and most of Pompey's army had already left by ship. Pompey, with twenty cohorts, remained in the city. Caesar invested the city from the landward side and started on a project to block the narrow harbor entrance. His engineers began to build moles in the shallow water on either side. These were to be linked together by large rafts with towers containing catapults. This project was less than half completed when Pompey's transports returned on March 17.

Pompey ordered his men to embark in the transports in all

haste. That night Caesar received word from the inhabitants of Brundisium that Pompey was planning to leave. He ordered an immediate assault. His legionaries soon scaled the thinly defended walls and some entered the city. Dashing to the harbor they found Pompey's transports leaving. Seizing some boats at the waterfront, Caesar's men managed to capture two transports that had run into the moles in the darkness. Pompey and the rest of his army got safely away. When Caesar entered the city on March 18, Italy was his. He returned to Rome.

Caesar's Strategy

No one knew better than Julius Caesar that his rapid and almost bloodless conquest of Italy was merely the beginning of a bitter war with Pompey. Not only must he secure Italy, but he would also have to challenge Pompey at sea, and in Rome's overseas provinces as well. Pompey had gone to Dyrrachium, in Macedonia, only a short trip across the Adriatic Sea. He could return as rapidly as he had left, but he assuredly would not return until he had gathered and trained an army he could trust.

Without a fleet, Caesar could not move his own legions over to challenge Pompey. Consequently he decided that he would first move, as quickly as possible, to Spain, where Pompey had seven legions. By defeating them Caesar could protect himself against attack from the rear when he later moved eastward.

111

With luck he could secure Spain before Pompey could raise an army and return to Italy. Spain also had the geographical advantage of being next to Gaul and easily reached by Caesar's loyal legions in Gaul.

Before leaving Italy, Caesar reassembled as much of the Senate as he could at Rome. He left Marcus Aemilius Lepidus as *praefectus urbi* to represent him in Rome during his absence; he put Mark Antony in general charge of the rest of Italy. Having seized the treasury in Rome, Caesar ordered shipwrights in the coastal towns to build a new fleet. He also sent Quintus Valerius with a legion to occupy Sardinia, and Curio with two more to take Sicily and the Roman province of Africa (Tunisia). Control of these provinces would help ensure an adequate supply of grain for Rome despite the ability of Pompey's fleet to cut off sea traffic to Italy. Sardinia and Sicily were secured without resistance, but Africa remained in the hands of Pompey's supporters.

With affairs in order at Rome, Caesar left for Massilia (Marseilles). He is reputed to have said: "I am going to fight an army without a leader, so that later I can fight a leader without an army." When he arrived at Massilia, about April 19, the garrison, made up of Pompey's troops, refused to let him enter. Domitius arrived by sea soon afterward and took command of the garrison in the city.

Control of Massilia was vital, for it lay on both land and sea lines of communication to Spain, so Caesar decided to besiege it. He ordered Decimus Brutus to build a fleet and to blockade Massilia from the sea. He placed Gaius Trebonius with three legions in command of the land siege. He then hurried on to Spain with a small escort.

Situation in Northern Spain

Six legions from Gaul, commanded by Gaius Fabius, had preceded Caesar into northern Spain. With 7,000 cavalry and 5,000 light auxiliaries, the total strength of the force was about 40,000 men. Caesar joined them near Ilerda (Lérida), north of the Iberus (Ebro) River, where five of Pompey's seven Spanish legions were assembled. Overall command of the Pompeian force was exercised by Lucius Afranius. Marcus Petreius, who commanded two of the legions, was second-in-command. In addition to the legions, Afranius and Petreius had a few cohorts of Iberian troops and 5,000 cavalry. The two armies were about equal in numbers.

Ilerda, a rocky hilltop town, was on the right bank of the swift Sicoris (Segre) River, which flows south into the Iberus. A stone bridge built across the river near the town was held by Afranius' troops. The remainder of the Pompeian infantry was encamped on a hill about a mile south of Ilerda, with the cavalry between the hill and the river.

When Fabius arrived from Gaul, he bridged the river in two places, one about 3 miles above Ilerda, the other some 4 miles farther up the river. He apparently built his camp on the west bank, about 4 miles from that of Afranius.

There was a shortage of food on the west bank, the Pom-

113

peian forces having gathered all they could find in a supply base in Ilerda. Shortly before Caesar arrived, early in June, Fabius sent foragers, protected by two legions, east of the river, to find urgently needed provisions. The force had hardly crossed the lower bridge when the river, swollen by rains, washed the bridge away. When Afranius saw the bridge timbers coming down the river, he at once crossed the stone bridge with four legions and his cavalry to attack the isolated force. But Fabius sent two more legions across the upper bridge, and, although there was a fierce cavalry action, both sides withdrew without a full-scale battle.

Ilerda Campaign

When Caesar arrived he promptly marched his entire army south toward the hill on which Afranius was encamped and offered battle on the plain below. But Afranius refused the challenge. Caesar then had his men build an entrenched camp on the plain below Afranius' camp. When the 15-foot-wide trench around the campsite had been completed, he moved the army's baggage from the old camp.

Caesar next tried to occupy a ridge that lay between the city and Afranius' camp. But Afranius rushed troops to the ridge, and after a five-hour fight, his troops retained control. He built entrenchments along the slopes, which discouraged Caesar from making another attempt.

Two days later, both of Caesar's bridges above Ilerda were

washed out. This made it impossible to send foragers to the east bank. More seriously, soon after this a large convoy of supplies and reinforcements for Caesar arrived from Gaul, approaching the river from the east. While this force was vainly seeking some way to reach Caesar's camp, it was attacked by Afranius and driven away from the river.

Since Afranius' troops now controlled the east bank of the river near Ilerda, Caesar could not rebuild his bridges, and his supply situation became more serious. Finally, at a point 22 miles above his camp, he sent a small party of men across the river in boats to establish an entrenched bridgehead. He built a bridge there, and sent more troops across the river to the bridgehead camp. From there Caesar's cavalry raided southward, cutting off and capturing great numbers of Pompeian foragers and their supplies. Afranius and his men were surprised by this unexpected foray of Caesar's troops on the east bank. Caesar also made contact with the convoy from Gaul, which joined the army.

Word now reached Caesar that the new ships of Decimus Brutus had defeated the fleet of Domitius at Massilia. The news spread rapidly through northern Spain, increasing Caesar's prestige. A number of towns and tribes in the Ilerda area joined his cause and agreed to supply him with grain. This greatly eased Caesar's supply situation.

Next, Caesar decided to establish a secure means of crossing the river near his camp. He put his troops to work constructing a ford near Ilerda. He did this by drawing off water from the river into ditches, 30 feet wide, dug at right angles to the

115

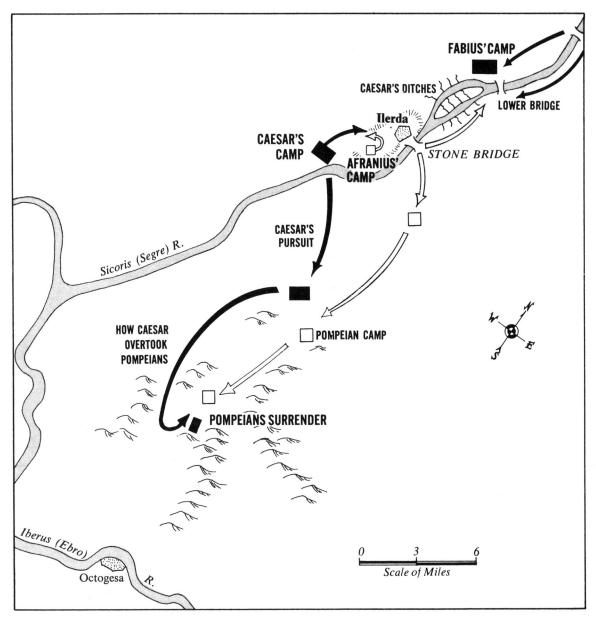

FABIUS' CAMP

CAESAR'S DITCHES

LOWER BRIDGE

Ilerda

STONE BRIDGE

CAESAR'S CAMP

AFRANIUS' CAMP

Sicoris (Segre) R.

CAESAR'S PURSUIT

HOW CAESAR OVERTOOK POMPEIANS

POMPEIAN CAMP

POMPEIANS SURRENDER

Iberus (Ebro)

Octogesa R.

0   3   6
Scale of Miles

The Ilerda Campaign.

stream along the banks and in an island in the river. Seeing this activity, Afranius decided to leave Ilerda and to move south of the Iberus, where tribes were still friendly to Pompey.

Since there was no bridge over the Iberus, Afranius sent word to the tribes along the river to gather all available boats and barges at the town of Octogesa (Ribarroja), and make a floating bridge across the river. Octogesa was 27 miles south of Ilerda, east of the Sicoris. In preparation for the march, Afranius and Petreius sent two legions across the stone bridge to build a camp on the east side of the Sicoris and south of the Iberus. The route from there to Octogesa was fairly level for about 12 miles, then became quite hilly, and for the last 8 miles was mountainous.

Caesar learned of these plans, and rushed work on the ford. By the time Afranius and Petreius started to march out of Ilerda, on July 25, the depth of the water had been reduced sufficiently for cavalry to cross. The infantry volunteered to cross also. Caesar approved. Two lines of pack animals were stretched across the stream above them to help break the force of the swift-flowing water. He then led his entire army across the stream, with the infantry wading through water shoulder deep.

As soon as his legions were safely on the east bank, Caesar sent his cavalry in pursuit of the Pompeians. Soon they were harassing the rear and flanks of the enemy column as it hurried toward the hills. Finally the Pompeians stopped and encamped, intending to push on again after dark.

Caesar soon arrived with his infantry, and camped on a hill

117

not far from that of Afranius. By questioning prisoners, he learned of the Pompeian plan to march that night. At dusk Caesar ordered a trumpet sounded, calling his men to form in columns and to prepare to march out. The trumpet was heard by Afranius and Petreius. Since they did not wish a night battle, they countermanded their own march orders and spent the night in their camp. While his patrols circled the Pompeian camp, Caesar also let most of his men return to their tents.

Both forces remained in camp the next day, while their commanders sent out scouts to reconnoiter the country. Afranius and Petreius decided to continue their withdrawal toward Octogesa. They prepared their men secretly for a rapid march, leaving a rear guard to block Caesar's pursuit. In this way they expected to reach the hilly country before Caesar could catch up with them.

The sudden departure of the Pompeians surprised Caesar; he immediately started to pursue, only to discover that the road in front of him was blocked. He decided to try another, longer route and to attempt to reach the hills before the enemy by faster marching. Caesar's legions succeeded in moving very rapidly across rough country and finally reached the road again, where it crossed a plain between two hills. Their efforts were successful; they arrived just before the Pompeians. Caesar quickly drew his troops up in line across the road. When Afranius came to the top of the hill overlooking the plain, and saw Caesar's army lined up across the road, he was amazed. He halted his troops and built a camp on the hill. Caesar immediately encamped on the plain below.

The two camps were within speaking distance and in the next two days soldiers of both sides were shouting back and forth to each other in friendly fashion. A few even crossed from one camp to the other. Petreius ended this friendly visiting by rounding up all of Caesar's men he could find in his camp, and slaughtering them. Caesar, however, sent the visitors to his camp back unharmed.

Supplies in the Pompeian camp soon ran out, and Afranius and Petreius decided to try to get back to Ilerda. On July 30 they started out. But they were so harassed by Caesar's cavalry that they went only 4 miles before they stopped on top of a hill.

After Caesar encamped nearby, the Pompeians started on again, only to be pursued and finally compelled to encamp in an unfavorable spot. When Caesar immediately started to build a contravallation trench, Afranius and Petreius lined up their troops for battle. Caesar marched his men out also but declined to attack. He had said repeatedly that if possible he wished to avoid the shedding of more Roman blood. Finally both sides withdrew to their camps. Caesar continued construction of his siege lines through the night.

Consolidation of Spain, Massilia, and Cisalpine Gaul

On August 2 the Pompeians recognized that their situation was hopeless. Afranius offered to surrender, and requested merciful terms. In reply Caesar merely demanded that the Pompeian army should be disbanded. The terms were im-

119

mediately accepted. By his generosity Caesar won greater respect in Spain and in Rome than if he had beaten the Pompeians in battle, as he could easily have done, or if he had insisted upon harsh punishment of the surrendered troops.

There still remained two Pompeian legions under Varro in Further Spain. Caesar sent Quintus Cassius Longinus there with two legions, and he secured Varro's surrender without a fight. Caesar then called for a general assembly of Roman administrators and tribal chiefs at Corduba. By the time he reached Corduba, the entire province of Iberia had submitted to his control, and he was acclaimed by the assembly.

Thus Spain had been won, with scarcely a battle. It remained only for Caesar to assign Cassius with four legions to govern the province. Then Caesar proceeded to Gades and sailed for Tarraco (Tarragona). From there he went by land to Massilia, arriving late in September. He was just in time to direct final action of the siege, and to accept the surrender of the city. He spared it, "because of its high antiquity and ancient renown." But he demanded the contents of its treasury and all its ships. He left two legions behind as a garrison and then continued on to Rome.

Another problem caused Caesar to halt at Placentia. Four of his legions had escorted the legionaries of Afranius and Petreius to the border of Transalpine Gaul, where the men were dispersed. Then the legions had been ordered to march back to Placentia, in the Po Valley. At the end of this march the troops were tired, having marched to and from Spain, and having conducted the active Ilerda campaign there, in a space of a few months.

But what bothered the troops most was the fact that they had little to show for their exertions. This new Caesar, with his policy of kindness and pity on the defeated, had given them little of the booty they had been accustomed to get after a victory. The 9th Legion, in particular, was on the verge of mutiny, when Caesar arrived to take charge of the situation.

The townspeople quaked, for they and the troops thought Caesar would give the legions permission to plunder the area where they were. Instead, Caesar announced that he would punish the 9th Legion with decimation—the execution of one out of every ten men. This threat of the maximum penalty caused the men to beg Caesar for mercy. In the end he relented a little, and only 12 of the leaders were executed, instead of the 300 that would have been killed by decimation. (By this time most of Caesar's legions had been reduced in strength to 3,000 men or less.)

CHAPTER 8

Dyrrachium and Pharsalus

Across the Adriatic

When Caesar returned to Rome, late in 49 B.C., it was as dictator under the old Roman law providing for one-man rule in times of danger. He had arranged the appointment through Aemilius Lepidus in order to retain his authority and thus assure his election as consul for the following year. There was some doubt about the constitutionality of the appointment, but no one dared dispute it. Caesar held consular elections soon after his return, and he and Publius Servilius were elected. Caesar retained the dictatorship for eleven days, during which he took action to improve public and private economic conditions in Rome, restored civil rights to the families who had been deprived of them by Sulla, and appointed magistrates and provincial governors.

The most important political, economic, and social problems in Rome disposed of, Caesar resigned the dictatorship and turned the government for the rest of the year back to the Senate. He hastened to join the twelve legions he had assembled at Brundisium. Pompey by this time had had nine months in

122

which to build up and train an army. Caesar could not afford to wait long before seeking a showdown.

Pompey had prepared himself well. In Macedonia and Greece he had recruited nine small legions of Roman citizens, filled out with large numbers of Greek soldiers. His total strength by the end of 49 B.C. was about 36,000 infantry, 7,000 cavalry, 3,000 archers, and 1,200 slingers. He had acquired ample funds from Asia, Syria, and Greece, and a large supply of grain from Egypt, Thessaly, and Asia. From all around the Eastern Mediterranean he had assembled a great fleet of more than 300 ships.

Although Caesar's shipbuilding program had been effective, while he was en route home from Spain 40 vessels had been lost. Caius Cornelius Dolabella, who commanded Caesar's fleet in the Adratic, had been badly defeated in an encounter with a squadron of Pompey's ships. So Caesar, who had decided to pursue Pompey to Macedonia and Greece, did not have enough ships to take all his army with him. He could have waited for spring, when more vessels could be available. Pompey in fact did not expect that he would risk his army on the wintry seas.

But Caesar believed that delay would work to Pompey's advantage, and that the calmer seas would increase the risk of encountering Pompey's fleet as Caesar's transports crossed the Adriatic. It was preferable to cross as soon as possible. He planned to take advantage of the first day of good weather, for the crossing took only one day.

On January 4, 48 B.C., Caesar set sail, with a fair wind that carried him with seven legions, about 15,000 soldiers, and 500 cavalry, safely across to Palaeste (Palissa), on the coast of Epirus. He sent the transports back at once to Brundisium to pick up the rest of the army, left under Antony's command. But by this time M. Calpurnius Bibulus, who had been about 50 miles away with 110 of Pompey's ships, had learned what was going on. He managed to capture and burn 30 of Caesar's transports on their way back to Brundisium.

The remainder of the transports reached port and embarked as many of Antony's troops as they could carry. Hardly had they set sail, however, when word was received from Caesar that the coast of Epirus was completely controlled by Bibulus and they should not attempt to join him. The convoy returned to Brundisium and Antony awaited further word from Caesar.

Negotiations and Maneuvers

Despite his great numerical disadvantage, Caesar made no attempt to conceal his whereabouts or his strength from Pompey. Instead he sent Vibullius Rufus, whom he had taken prisoner in Spain, to Pompey on a mission of peace. Caesar proposed that they call on the Senate and Roman people to make peace and that both men swear a public oath to disband their armies within three days.

Caesar then seized Oricum, farther up the coast, which he made his main base. Leaving a legion there, he went on to Apollonia, which also opened its gates to him. Other nearby

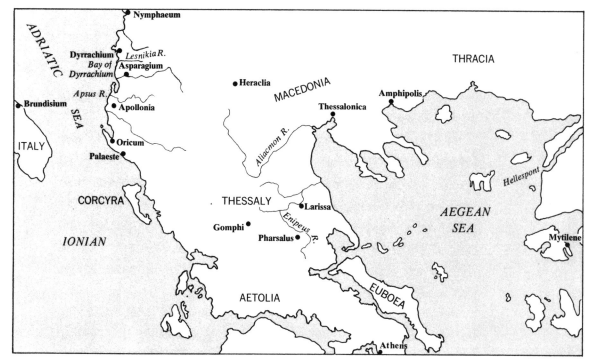

Theater of Dyrrachium-Pharsalus Campaign.

communities followed suit. Then he marched at top speed toward Dyrrachium, where Pompey had his main supply depot.

Vibullius, meanwhile, had ridden as fast as he could to Pompey, to deliver Caesar's message. Also, as a good officer, Vibullius reported on Caesar's whereabouts, and the exact conditon of his army. Pompey had been marching slowly from his training grounds in Macedonia toward winter quarters around Apollonia and Dyrrachium. He immediately increased his speed, reaching Dyrrachium before Caesar. He deployed his troops near the city, to block off Caesar's approach on the road from Apollonia.

125

When he reached Pompey's lines, Caesar decided to fall back and await the arrival of his other legions. He encamped on the southern bank of the Apsus (Semani) River. Pompey then made his camp on the opposite bank.

So close were the armies that the men could talk with one another across the river. Caesar attempted to use this means to discuss peace. It came to naught, however, for Labienus, who had deserted Caesar when he crossed the Rubicon, became engaged in a loud argument with one of Caesar's officers. All talk of peace came to an end when Labienus shouted: "Cease then to talk about a settlement, for there can be no peace for us till Caesar's head is brought in!"

Pompey's ships continued to patrol the coast and, as spring approached, became even more active. But Caesar was getting impatient. In response to his urging, Antony finally set sail from Italy with four legions and 800 cavalry. With a good following breeze the fleet sailed past Dyrrachium, where it was sighted. A Pompeian squadron put to sea and chased it up the coast. But a fortunate change of wind permitted Antony to land in safety at Nymphaeum (San Giovanni di Medua), while 16 of Pompey's ships were driven on the rocks and wrecked.

News of Antony's arrival reached Pompey before it got to Caesar. Pompey at once set out to cut off and surprise Antony. But Antony was alert, and his troops were lined up in battle formation. When Pompey learned that Caesar was following him, he abandoned his plan and moved to Asparagium, leaving the way open for Caesar to join Antony. Caesar now had nearly 30,000 men.

About this time Caesar learned that a contingent of troops, under Metellus Scipio, was marching from Syria through Macedonia to join Pompey. Caesar sent a force under Domitius Calvinus to intercept Scipio. He also sent another legion into Thessaly, and five cohorts to Aetolia to procure grain. These detachments greatly weakened Caesar's army, and particularly his garrison at Oricum. Pompey's son Gnaeus, in command of a squadron of ships that had been sent from Egypt, entered the harbor at Oricum and destroyed or seized all of the galleys that were there. He then sailed to Nymphaeum and destroyed all of Antony's ships. Caesar was left without even a ship with which to communicate with Italy.

Caesar meanwhile had marched toward Asparagium and camped not far from Pompey. Despite his great numerical superiority, Pompey refused to accept a challenge to fight. So Caesar decided to try once more to seize Dyrrachium. In order to get around Pompey, who was camped between him and his objective, Caesar took a long route. By fast marching he managed to reach the road approaching Dyrrachium about an hour before Pompey's legions appeared. Caesar encamped beside the sea on the north side of a small, fast stream; Pompey entrenched just south of it, and ordered a squadron of ships to the little harbor of Petra.

Caesar was at a disadvantage, although he sat between Pompey and his storehouse at Dyrrachium. Caesar's army was entirely dependent on the territory for supplies, but since little food was grown in this rough and hilly area, he had to forage aggressively. But Pompey, who had superior cavalry, harassed

127

this foraging effort constantly. Pompey, on the other hand, having command of the sea, could be supplied by ship from his stores in Dyrrachium. Caesar, moveover, lacked the strength and the equipment to attack the strongly defended city, particularly when he had to hold Pompey off at the same time.

Blockade of Dyrrachium

When it was clear that Pompey was unwilling to fight, Caesar decided to try to blockade his army, which occupied some 5 miles of the shore of the Bay of Dyrrachium. First he began to fortify the hilltops in an arc around Pompey's army. He planned to join these strong places with entrenchments, to pen the enemy in. This would confine Pompey's cavalry and give his own more freedom to graze and to forage. Furthermore, it would reduce Pompey's prestige by making it clear that he did not dare fight. As soon as Pompey realized what was going on, he too set to work to fortify as many hills as possible, to force Caesar to build his line longer and farther away.

Work on both lines proceeded, with much skirmishing as both sides tried to gain control of the most strategic spots. Caesar's food supply became critical. But Pompey also had his troubles; his pack animals began to die of starvation as all the available fodder was given to the cavalry horses. When Caesar dammed the mountain streams to deprive Pompey of water, his men dug wells near the coast. These dried up, however, and to save his horses Pompey shipped them all by sea to Dyrrachium.

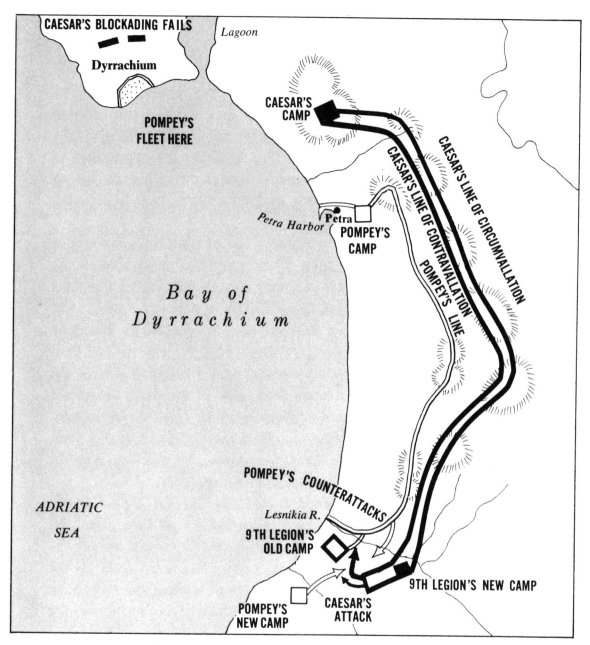

CAESAR'S BLOCKADING FAILS

Lagoon

Dyrrachium

POMPEY'S FLEET HERE

CAESAR'S CAMP

CAESAR'S LINE OF CIRCUMVALLATION

CAESAR'S LINE OF CONTRAVALLATION

POMPEY'S LINE

Petra Harbor

Petra

POMPEY'S CAMP

B a y o f
D y r r a c h i u m

POMPEY'S COUNTERATTACKS

ADRIATIC

SEA

Lesnikia R.

9 TH LEGION'S OLD CAMP

9TH LEGION'S NEW CAMP

POMPEY'S NEW CAMP

CAESAR'S ATTACK

Operations around Dyrrachium.

Caesar made one attempt to take Dyrrachium, apparently vainly expecting it to be betrayed to him. During his absence Pompey's men made three attacks on Caesar's contravallation lines, but were beaten off. After the failure of his effort to take the city, Caesar built two forts blocking the approaches to Dyrrachium so that Pompey's cavalry could not go out to forage. This forced Pompey to shift his horses back to his camp and supply them by sea.

The southern end of Caesar's line of contravallation was in the valley of the Lesnikia River, south of Pompey's camp. As the line was being built, Caesar's men also worked on a parallel line of circumvallation about 600 yards behind, to protect the garrisons from attack from the rear. He planned to join these two lines by a wall along the shore. Pompey's line too had been turned westward toward the sea, on the northern side of the Lesnikia. Between the two lines, south of the river, was an old camp that had been used temporarily by Caesar's 9th Legion, which had now moved to a camp between Caesar's double lines. Pompey occupied the old camp and he built a wall from it northeastward to the river to protect its water supply.

When Pompey learned from some deserters from Caesar's army that the two lines of defenses had not yet been joined, he devised a plan of attack. He would send 60 cohorts against the line of contravallation from the north, close to the coast. At the same time he would land lightly armed soldiers and archers by sea between the ends of the two lines and also behind the circumvallation.

Pompey's attack began at daybreak on July 10 and took the defenders completely by surprise. The attackers soon pushed up between the lines and the defenders fled inland. Before Pompey's men could attack the new camp of the 9th Legion, however, Antony came up with twelve cohorts and drove them back. Then Caesar, with thirteen more cohorts, drove them on within a mile of the coast. At that point he halted and joined his two lines of defense walls.

Pompey meanwhile had built another camp south of the second line, so that his cavalry and his foragers could go through from the plain south of the Lesnikia. This enabled him to retain control of the coastline, and prevented Caesar from extending his works to the shore.

Caesar decided to attack the 9th Legion's old camp, which Pompey was occupying, south of the Lesnikia. With thirty-three cohorts in two columns he advanced through the woods toward the camp. The left column attacked the eastern side of the camp, while the right, coming up to the rampart Pompey had built, followed along it north to the riverbank. There the soldiers broke through and entered the plain above the camp.

Pompey at once marched from the south with five legions toward the camp, while his cavalry rode onto the plain east of the camp and threatened the rear of the right column. Caesar's men panicked. Unable to withdraw because of the rampart, they climbed over the wall, many perishing as they tried to escape. Caesar's left column had driven back the garrison as it entered the camp, but when Pompey came up, the garrison turned and counterattacked. The men of Caesar's left column saw their companions of the right turn and flee and they too panicked. Despite Caesar's attempts to rally them, the soldiers ran from the field in complete disorder. Fortunately Pompey did not pursue. He had gained a clear victory, although only a portion of Caesar's army was engaged.

Caesar now realized that it would be impossible for his smaller army, inadequately supplied, to accomplish anything by besieging Pompey's larger, well-supplied force. In fact, by continuing the effort he would risk disaster. So he decided to move to a place where he could find food for his army, rest his men, and restore their morale. He went to Apollonia, where he could care for his numerous sick and wounded. Although Pompey followed as soon as he learned of the movement, Caesar managed to elude him and reach Apollonia without interference.

Into Thessaly

After considering what Pompey might do and what he himself should do, Caesar decided that he must march to join Domitius Calvinus, who had been sent to keep Scipio from crossing Macedonia to join Pompey. He started eastward.

Pompey learned of the movement, and was not sure what he should do. He was inclined to follow Caesar, cutting off his supplies, while avoiding battle. But Pompey's decision was complicated by the fact that he still had with him a group of senators, knights, and officials who had no responsibility for the fighting, and who were interested only in their own futures. All, however, were eager to give Pompey advice. Most of them insisted that Pompey should go to the aid of Scipio, even if this required a battle. Still not sure, Pompey slowly followed Caesar eastward.

Domitius by this time was at Heraclia (Zervokhori), foraging. He had not had any recent word from Caesar. Learning that Pompey was approaching, Domitius at once moved south to the valley of the Aliacmon River. There, apparently by chance, he joined Caesar.

Word of Pompey's victory at Dyrrachium had spread through Thessaly. The towns which earlier had sent envoys to Caesar had by this time turned toward what appeared to be the winning side. When Caesar approached Gomphi (Paleo-Episkopi), heading south, the gates were closed. He stormed the town and then, as an example to other towns, permitted his men to plunder it. Apparently this worked; all other Thessalian towns submitted to Caesar thereafter. South of the Enipeus River, Caesar found a place where the crops were abundant, and the terrain seemed to him suitable for a battle. This was either Pharsalus (Fersala) or Palaepharsalus (Mt. Koutouri), towns about 7 miles apart. There he camped to await the arrival of Pompey, who he knew was following him.

Pompey joined Scipio at Larissa and then marched 20 miles into the Enipeus Valley to encamp on the slopes of a hill facing Caesar's camp, about 3½ miles away. Although his army was much smaller, Caesar at once marched his army out and challenged Pompey to battle. But Pompey would not move down into the plain. Instead he formed his line on the slopes near his camp, where Caesar's outnumbered men would have to attack uphill. Caesar would not tempt fortune to that extent.

Caesar tried for several days to provoke battle on the plain, but only a few calvary skirmishes resulted. Supplies were beginning to run low, so he decided to break camp and move to a new location with more food. Furthermore, movement would also tire Pompey's men, who were not in such good physical condition as his own. And in a new location, perhaps, there would be a better opportunity to fight on favorable terms.

On August 9, 48 B.C., Caesar ordered his troops to strike their tents and prepare to move out. But as the head of the column was about to leave the camp, Caesar noticed that Pompey had moved his men out of camp and farther down into the plain than he had on any previous day. Caesar decided that this was too good an opportunity to miss. He ordered his men to drop their baggage and to prepare for battle. In a few minutes he marched them out in battle line, leaving a small contingent to guard the camp.

Pompey's Battle Plan

Pompey apparently had been persuaded by the self-appointed advisers in his camp that he should change his tactics and attack. He had 45,000 infantry and 6,700 cavalry to oppose

Caesar's 22,000 infantry and 1,000 cavalry. Pompey realized that Caesar's veteran legionaries were better than his own. But he believed that his great numerical advantage more than offset this qualitative difference.

Furthermore, Pompey knew that his cavalry was much better than Caesar's, as well as being much more numerous. He intended to make decisive use of his horsemen in his battle plan. As soon as the armies drew near to each other, Pompey planned to throw his cavalry in a swift charge against Caesar's right wing, then swing around and attack Caesar's main body from the rear. Pompey was confident that this would throw Caesar's troops into such confusion that they would flee; his own legions might well never become involved in the fight at all.

Pompey himself commanded his left wing, made up of five legions, including the two that had been sent from Gaul to Rome. Scipio with his two legions was in the center. The right wing was commanded by Lentulus who had four legions, plus some cohorts under Afranius, who had joined Pompey after leaving Spain. All the legions were in the normal three-line formation, each line ten men deep. Pompey's right flank was protected by the river. On his left he had concentrated in his main striking force all of his cavalry, archers, and slingers under the command of Labienus.

Caesar's Plans

Caesar placed the 10th Legion under Publius Sulla on his right flank; the 9th and 8th Legions were on the left, commanded by Antony. Domitius Calvinus commanded the five legions in the center. Caesar took his own post in the rear of the 10th Legion, since he realized that the main action would take place on the right. His men were also in three lines, but, in order to match the length of Pompey's front as closely as possible, they were probably only five or six men deep. Also, Caesar placed his third line farther back from the other two lines than was the normal Roman custom. His small cavalry contingent was on the right of the 10th Legion.

While his troops were forming for battle, Caesar observed Pompey's dispositions. He at once guessed Pompey's plan of attack. Consequently he withdrew one cohort each from the third line of six of his legions, and posted them behind the cavalry and the 10th Legion on his right, so that they would not be detected by the enemy. He formed these at an oblique angle to the front, prepared to meet Pompey's expected cavalry envelopment. He then ordered his trumpets to sound the charge.

Battle of Pharsalus

As Caesar's army came swiftly across the plain, Pompey ordered his men to stand fast so that they would not be breathless when the battle was joined. In this way Caesar's troops, having had to run much farther than expected, would

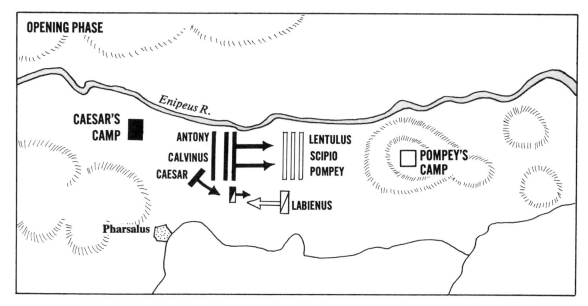

Battle of Pharsalus (opening phase).

be tired and somewhat disordered. But Caesar, realizing what Pompey had in mind, ordered another trumpet blast, stopping his men just beyond javelin range from Pompey's motionless line. After the troops had caught their breath, and had dressed their lines, Caesar again ordered the charge.

Once more Caesar's men proceeded at a run toward the waiting foe. At the appropriate point they hurled their javelins. Pompey's men hurled theirs at almost the same instant. Then both sides fell to with their swords.

As soon as the two lines were engaged, Labienus and his cavalry charged at Caesar's right, closely followed by the archers and slingers. By its sheer weight the attack drove Caesar's cavalry back, and the enemy horsemen advanced against the exposed flank of the 10th Legion. To their surprise and shock,

137

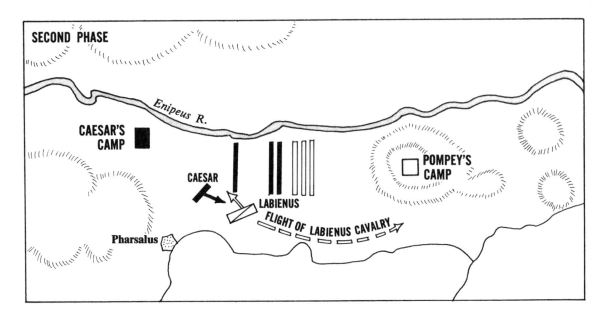

Battle of Pharsalus (second and third phases).

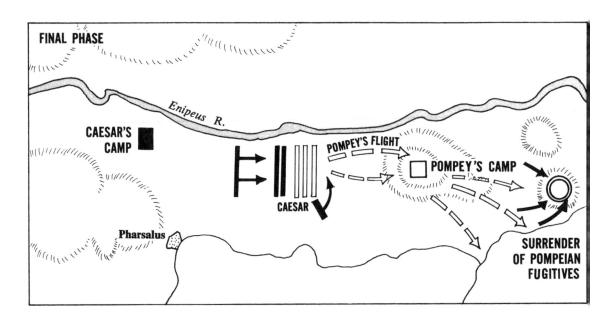

the attackers suddenly found themselves confronted by Caesar's special line of six cohorts. As the attackers hesitated, Caesar himself led this line of infantry in a counterattack. They hurled their javelins at the Pompeian cavalry, then charged. The surprised horsemen turned and fled, galloping off to safety in the hills. The archers and slingers behind them were trampled under the horses' hooves or slain by Caesar's onrushing soldiers.

Without halting, Caesar ordered the six cohorts to continue across the field and to swing behind Pompey's left flank. Meanwhile in the center both lines had held firm and fighting was fierce. Soon Caesar's first two lines and all three of Pompey's lines were engaged. Then Caesar, who had returned to direct the main battle, ordered his third line forward to relieve those at the front. Just as this fresh wave hit the fighting line, the six cohorts struck Pompey's legions from the rear. In confusion and disorder Pompey's men broke and fled. Pompey, seeing his whole army coming apart, rode back to camp.

Caesar pursued the disorganized enemy to the camp, but the fugitives continued their flight into the hills. After occupying the camp, Caesar resumed the pursuit with four legions. Most of the defeated Pompeians had taken refuge at the top of a nearby hill. Caesar cut them off from a stream at the base of the hill, their only water supply. This caused the defeated troops to surrender without further fight.

Pompey meanwhile had escaped from the camp just as Caesar's men were breaking through its defenses. With thirty horsemen he fled past Larissa on the coast, embarked on a ship, and sailed north to Amphipolis. From there he went to Mytilene, joining his wife and son, who had been living there.

139

CHAPTER 9

Alexandria and Zela—and Cleopatra

The Death of Pompey

Caesar did not take long to decide on his next move. He would follow Pompey. Stopping for a day at Larissa, Caesar sent Antony and a few legions back to assure control of Italy. He sent Domitius Calvinus to Asia, with three legions made up largely of troops that had just surrendered. Then, taking the 6th Legion and 800 cavalry, Caesar proceeded overland to the Hellespont.

From there, Caesar decided to continue the pursuit by water, since most of Pompey's fleet had surrendered after the Battle of Pharsalus. He sailed to Ephesus, then on to Rhodes, and finally set sail for Alexandria in Egypt. Somewhere along the way he was joined by Fufius Calenus and another legion, bringing his force to about 3,200 men. Caesar had been correctly informed that Pompey had gone to Rhodes and then on to Egypt, with about 2,000 troops.

Since the death of Alexander the Great, Egypt had been ruled by the Ptolemy Dynasty. About four years before the Battle

140

of Pharsalus, Ptolemy XI had died and passed the rule to two minors, Ptolemy XII and his brilliant sister Cleopatra VII. At the time of Pompey's arrival Cleopatra was twenty-one years old, her brother fourteen. Young Ptolemy's minister had conspired to gain sole control of the kingdom. This had led to a civil war and Cleopatra was driven to Syria. Recently she had returned, with an army. As Pompey approached Pelusium, near the eastern branch of the Nile, he found the two Egyptian armies encamped near each other. He asked Ptolemy for asylum, but was lured ashore and murdered on September 28, 48 B.C.

When Caesar arrived off Alexandria a few days later he was presented with the embalmed head of Pompey, at sight of which, says Plutarch, he was moved to tears.

Caesar and Cleopatra

With Pompey out of the way, Caesar might well have returned to Italy. But instead he decided to go ashore and settle the strife between Ptolemy and Cleopatra, because he believed the quarrel came under his jurisdiction as consul of Rome. In 59 B.C., the preceding Ptolemy had signed a treaty with Rome, and his will had called on Rome to see that his wishes were carried out. He had also promised Rome a large sum of money which had never been paid. Confirming Caesar's decision to intervene was the fact that the prevailing winds at that season made it almost impossible to sail from Alexandria.

141

Clearly Caesar expected to meet with no resistance, for he had with him only his two understrength legions. He stepped ashore at Alexandria like a conquering general, apparently assuming that his prestige was so great that the Egyptians would immediately acknowledge him as their master.

To Caesar's surprise, however, the Egyptian populace was enraged by this intervention in their affairs. Rioting broke out. Demonstrations during several days took the lives of many of Caesar's soldiers. Caesar moved into the royal palace beside the harbor and sent urgent messages to his subordinates in Greece and Asia Minor to send help. He ordered Domitius to send two legions, and instructed Mithridates of Pergamum—a Roman ally—to come with all the troops he could raise. From other quarters he summoned cavalry, archers, ships, and supplies. Despite his present weakness, however, Caesar boldly called on Ptolemy and Cleopatra to disband their armies and to settle their differences peaceably.

From Ptolemy, Caesar demanded payment of 10,000,000 drachmas, evidently the amount the former king had promised to pay as tribute to Rome. In response, Pothinus, the most influential of Ptolemy's advisers, told Caesar to go away, saying that he would get the money eventually. Caesar, insulted by this reply, now apparently decided to throw the power of Rome against Ptolemy XII. Secretly he sent for Cleopatra. Thereupon began one of the most famous love stories of all time.

Cleopatra landed from a small boat near the palace in the evening, accompained by a friend, Apollodorus. To get into the palace unseen, she told Apollodorus to wrap her in a coverlet, and to carry her on his back into Caesar's apartment, as though he were carrying a rug. Caesar, says Plutarch, "was first captivated by this proof of Cleopatra's bold wit, and was afterwards so overcome by the charm of her society that he made a reconciliation between her and her brother, on the condition that she should rule as his colleague." But the troubles did not end with this reconciliation.

Without Caesar's knowledge, Pothinus had ordered Achillas, commander in chief of Ptolemy's army, to move his forces from Pelusium to Alexandria. When Caesar heard that the Egyptian army was approaching he could do nothing with his own small band of men but try to hold the palace area. Achillas occupied the rest of the city.

Brink of Disaster in Alexandria

Opposite the harbor of Alexandria, and protecting it from the sea, lies the island of Pharos, on which stood a towering lighthouse that was one of the Seven Wonders of the Ancient World. At this time the island was joined to the mainland by a mole, which divided the harbor in two. The western part was known as the Harbor of Eunostus; the eastern, where the palace was, as the Great Harbor. Except for narrow channels, the entrances to both harbors were shallow.

There were 72 Egyptian warships in the Great Harbor, where Caesar had 34 galleys. Caesar seized the Egyptian ships, but since he had no sailors for them, he burned them to prevent

Achillas from using them. He also seized the lighthouse, and so controlled the entrance to the Great Harbor.

Achillas was murdered at about this time, by the younger sister of Cleopatra, Arsinoë, who had joined the Egyptian army and who had been proclaimed queen by Pothinus. Ganymedes, an able soldier, now was put in command of the Egyptian army. He promptly cut the conduits which brought fresh water to the palace area, and then poured sea water through them to the palace cisterns. Caesar's soldiers almost mutinied when they found that their water supply was ruined. But Caesar promptly solved the problem by sinking wells, which produced abundant water.

The 37th Legion, sent by Domitius, now arrived off Alexandria, but because of unfavorable winds had to anchor about 8 miles west of the Great Harbor. Caesar took his fleet of galleys, without soldiers, since he could not afford to reduce the garrison holding the palace, and rowed around to meet the convoy of reinforcements. After an encounter with the fleet of Ganymedes, which cost the Egyptians two ships, Caesar's galleys towed the troop transports to the Great Harbor.

Now that he had nearly 5,000 troops, Caesar decided to seize the initiative. He planned to occupy the entire island of Pharos and the mole between the harbors. He sent his fleet, commanded by the Rhodian admiral Euphranor, into the Eunostus harbor. The Romans rammed three Egyptian ships, sank two, and sent the rest scurrying to shelter.

Caesar then led an amphibious attack against the Egyptians holding the mole. The defenders were more stubborn than he expected, and the action lasted for two days. Just as success seemed in his grasp, Egyptian reinforcements arrived. The fresh troops overwhelmed the outnumbered and exhausted Romans, who withdrew to their ships. Caesar's ship capsized, and although he removed his purple garments, he was an obvious target for Egyptian missiles. Only because of his expertness as a swimmer did he escape.

Shortly after this, command of the Egyptians again changed. Upon the urging of Ptolemy's friends, Caesar released the Egyptian king, who promised to put an end to the fighting. But, once released, Ptolemy took command in the war against Caesar, although actual leadership was still exercised by Pothinus.

The Tide Changes

Not long after this, Mithridates of Pergamum arrived overland from the east with his army, in response to Caesar's request. He occupied Pelusium, after a day of fighting. He then led men up the eastern branch of the Nile toward modern Cairo, with the intention of turning back down the western branch. (The Nile delta was so cut up by canals and small branches of the river that it was impracticable to march straight across to Alexandria.) Ptolemy sent a detachment to block this move, but Mithridates defeated the Egyptians about 17 miles north of Cairo.

About this time Caesar and his small army sailed out of

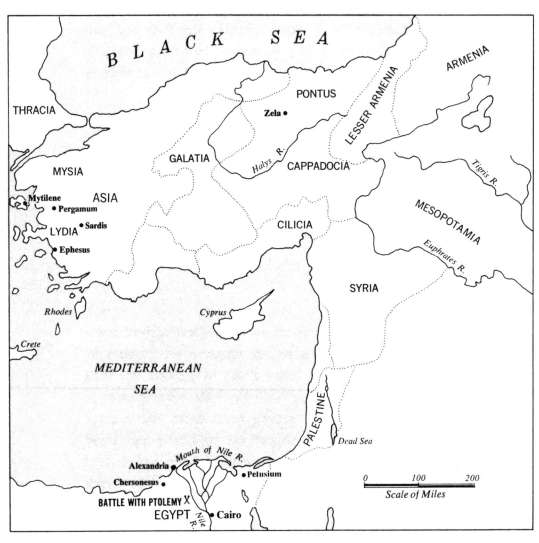

Operations in Egypt and Asia Minor.

Alexandria, heading east. Believing that Caesar had left to join Mithridates by sea, Ptolemy then set out by boat with his entire army, up the western branch of the river, intending to fight Mithridates before Caesar could arrive. At night, however, Caesar turned his fleet around and landed at Chersonesus, west of Alexandria. From there he marched rapidly by land up the western side of the Nile, and joined Mithridates northwest of Cairo before Ptolemy could get there by boat.

When he learned that Caesar and Mithridates had joined, Ptolemy camped in a strong position beside the Nile. The Egyptian camp was on a hill with easy access only from the river and one other side, and on that side a marsh added to the complications of approach.

Caesar first encountered Ptolemy's cavalry and some lightly armed troops at a canal some 7 miles from the Egyptian camp. The Egyptians succeeded in holding him back until his German cavalry found a place where the bank was not too steep and the water not too deep to cross. As the cavalry attacked on the flank, Caesar's infantry crossed the canal on trees they felled for the purpose. The Egyptian covering force withdrew, and Caesar moved on to Ptolemy's camp. By sending some troops to attack on the undefended side, Caesar caused such confusion in the camp that the defenders fled to the river. Ptolemy himself was drowned when his galley capsized.

Victorious Caesar hastened back to Alexandria, where the king's garrison begged for mercy. Thus Caesar became master in Egypt. He banished Arsinoë to Italy and put Ptolemy's younger brother on the throne as Ptolemy XIII to rule jointly

147

with Cleopatra. Then he spent two months sailing on the Nile with the lovely Egyptian queen, before quitting Alexandria in June of 47 B.C. He left three legions behind him to control the country.

Eight months had been spent in a diversion and a war that had nothing to do with the civil war. But before returning to Rome to tend to affairs there, Caesar decided to complete the pacification of the Eastern Mediterranean region. King Pharnaces of Pontus had taken advantage of the civil war, and of Caesar's stay in Egypt, to seize the Roman protectorates of Cappadocia and Lesser Armenia. Domitius Calvinus, whom Caesar had sent to Asia Minor after the Battle of Pharsalus, had tried to help the kings of those two states but had been severely defeated by Pharnaces.

"Veni, Vidi, Vici"

Caesar sailed from Alexandria for Syria and Cappadocia with about one thousand men. After brief stops in Syria and Cilicia, he joined Domitius in northern Cappadocia, or southern Galatia. With this small army he marched into Pontus and encamped 5 miles from Pharnaces' army near the town of Zela.

After reconnoitering, Caesar sent his men at night to seize a hill about a mile from the enemy, separated from Pharnaces' camp by a deep ravine. Caesar thought that this ravine made both camps unassailable on the sides facing the ravine.

At dawn the following day, August 2, Pharnaces drew up his army on the other side of the ravine. Then, while Caesar was wondering what Pharnaces' plan was, the king led his troops down the steep slope into the ravine and then rapidly up toward Caesar's undefended camp. Before Caesar could muster all his forces in battle line, the chariots of Pharnaces were upon them. Close behind came the Pontian foot soldiers.

Fighting was bitter, but at length the Roman legions pushed the attackers back down the slope and followed them through the ravine into their camp. Almost all of Pharnaces' army was either killed or captured. Caesar recorded this victory in three immortal words: *"Veni, vidi, vici*—'I came, I saw, I conquered!'"

Caesar promptly sent the 6th Legion back to Italy. But he remained for a while in Asia, settling disputes and organizing the administration of the states under Roman rule. Then at last he returned to Italy late in the summer of 47 B.C., a full year after his victory at Pharsalus.

Caesar has been criticized for wasting a year, doing nothing for the stabilization of the government in Rome, and nothing to end the civil war. This criticism is only partly fair. He was justified on military and political grounds to pursue Pompey, and in fact this pursuit resulted in Pompey's death, the most important step Caesar could have taken to end the civil war. He was also probably justified in stabilizing affairs in the Eastern Mediterranean region, before dealing with other enemies elsewhere. He had been rash in going to Egypt with too few troops and, despite his phenomenal luck—and skill—in emer-

149

ging from near disaster, this had probably led to unnecessary delay. His two-month dalliance with Cleopatra, of course, cannot be justified so easily. But Caesar probably needed the vacation.

CHAPTER 10

Final Campaigns in Africa and Spain

Restoring Order in Rome

Caesar once more returned to Rome as dictator. Antony had seen to it that he was named again to that post during his absence. Rome was full of unrest and problems, which Caesar speedily attacked. He took measures to bring financial relief to debtors; he filled vacancies in the Senate and held consular elections. He also raised a great deal of money to support further military operations, for he knew that he must go to Africa as soon as possible. During the time he had been occupied in Egypt and the Middle East, the supporters of Pompey in Africa had strengthened their position and built up their military force. Caesar had to remove this threat.

Caesar's soldiers in Italy well knew that he would soon be going to Africa, and that he was dependent on them. They were very unhappy because they had never received the prize money he promised them before Pharsalus, and because they had been in service for many years longer than they had expected. Mu-

151

tiny broke out among the legions stationed in Campania Caesar sent the historian Sallust with a promise to pay them a bounty after the campaign in Africa, but the troops stoned Sallust. They then marched to Rome and camped outside the city on the Campus Martius.

Caesar, apprehensive of what the mutineers might do next, took precautions to protect the city and his own house, then went boldly out to confront the men. They were surprised to see him appear among them without guard or protection. They were even more surprised when he assembled them and asked simply, "What do you want?" Feeling secure in their knowledge that they were indispensable to Caesar, they said, "We wish to be disbanded."

"I discharge you," replied Caesar. "And I will give you all that I have promised you when I have conquered with others." When he then addressed them as "Quirites ('citizens')!" they were stunned, for this meant that they would have no part of the rich booty to be won in Africa. They pleaded to be taken back, and Caesar accepted them, assured that they would give him no more trouble.

Three of Pompey's men—Metellus Scipio, Labienus, and Afranius—had gone to Utica, capital of the Roman province in Africa (modern Tunisia) after the defeat at Pharsalus. There others had joined them, including Pompey's two sons, Gnaeus and Sextus. Scipio had assumed command of the army, and Cato had been installed as governor of Utica. Juba, king of Numidia, had accepted the authority of the Pompeians, and agreed to join his army with theirs.

Juba had four legions—about 20,000 men, plus 18,000 cavalrymen, numerous light troops, and about 120 elephants. Scipio had about 50,000 men, organized in ten legions, plus 1,600 horsemen, and miscellaneous lightly armed soldiers. The large numbers were important, for the Pompeians knew that the quality of these forces was not high in comparison to Caesar's veterans.

To Africa

Caesar ordered the assembly of his army at Lilybaeum in Sicily. By December 25 he had six legions, of which two were veterans, and about 2,000 cavalry—probably about 20,000 men in all. Impatient to be off, he set sail, leaving orders that other troops, as they arrived, were to be sent to join him as soon as possible.

In three days Caesar arrived off the port of Hadrumetum (Susa), with about 3,000 infantry and 150 cavalry. The rest of the fleet was nowhere in sight, and he had apparently neglected to tell the captains of the other ships where to meet. Thus only by chance could he expect to see them again. He hastily sent ships back to Sardinia and Sicily for more men and supplies and ordered ten ships to go out and look for the missing transports.

Caesar rested his men for a day near Hadrumetum and then moved on to Ruspina (Monastir), where the inhabitants welcomed him. At Leptis too he was well received. There some of

153

the missing ships appeared. A few days later the remainder appeared at Ruspina just as he was about to set out to look for them personally.

The Numidian horsemen of the Pompeians had already begun to harass Caesar's small force, and he recognized that it would be difficult to protect troops he sent out foraging to sustain his army. Caesar led the first major foraging expedition himself, with about half of his army—30 cohorts, all of his cavalry, and about 150 archers. He encountered Labienus with 1,600 Gallic and Germanic horsemen, 8,000 Numidian horsemen, and at least 20,000 assorted foot soldiers.

Battle of Ruspina

Labienus knew that despite numerical superiority he would stand little chance in a formal battle and so determined to try to encircle Caesar's cohorts, to cut them off from their camp, and then bombard them with missiles. He placed the Numidian cavalry in the center, interspersed with light troops and archers, and posted his other cavalry on the flanks. Caesar drew up his little army in a single, long line, with cavalry on the wings and archers in front.

Labienus' cavalry rushed forward on both wings and forced Caesar's cavalry back. In the center of the line Labienus employed his horses in the Numidian tactics of charging, retreating, and charging again, tactics that threw Caesar's men into confusion. Meanwhile the flanks of Labienus' line had moved around to encircle Caesar's army completely.

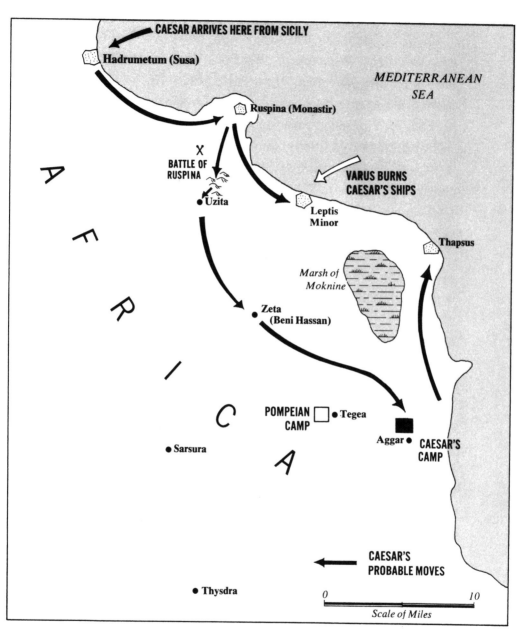

CAESAR ARRIVES HERE FROM SICILY

Hadrumetum (Susa)

MEDITERRANEAN
SEA

Ruspina (Monastir)

X
BATTLE OF
RUSPINA

VARUS BURNS
CAESAR'S SHIPS

Uzita

Leptis
Minor

Thapsus

*Marsh of
Moknine*

Zeta
(Beni Hassan)

A F R I C A

POMPEIAN
CAMP

Tegea

Aggar

CAESAR'S
CAMP

Sarsura

CAESAR'S
PROBABLE MOVES

Thysdra

0   10
Scale of Miles

Caesar in Africa

Caesar's situation was desperate. Somehow he rallied his men and drew them up in two lines, back to back. The two lines then attacked away from each other. On both sides they pushed the enemy back, until there was space enough between his lines for Caesar to form up two counterattacking forces. In a coordinated charge, these two forces broke through the encirclement, and Caesar rapidly withdrew through the gap toward the nearby hills. Marcus Petreius and Calpurnius Piso rode up with 1,600 more Numidian cavalry and attacked his rear, but Caesar's cavalry drove them off.

After resting and reorganizing his troops in the hills, Caesar marched back to his camp at Ruspina and set his men to work strengthening the defenses. It was now clear that the task of pacifying Africa would be more difficult than he had expected. He sent urgent messages to Italy and Sicily for reinforcements and supplies, for he was too weak to move from Ruspina and was not secure from a direct attack.

Scipio and the main Pompeian army arrived shortly after the engagement and camped about 3 miles from Caesar, beside Petreius and Labienus. Daily the Pompeians sent cavalry to harass Caesar's foragers and almost daily Scipio drew up his battle line to challenge Caesar. Juba, with large numbers of horsemen and foot soldiers, was on his way to join them when he got word that two rival kings had attacked some towns in Numidia. He left and took with him some men he had earlier loaned to Scipio.

Late in January, 46 B.C., a convoy arrived bringing Caesar two legions (the 13th and 14th) plus about 800 Gallic cavalry,

1,000 archers and slingers, and large supplies of grain. With this additional strength he felt he could challenge his opponents. Moreover, penned in as he had been, he was running short of fodder for his horses.

During the night of January 25–26 Caesar set out south from his camp at Ruspina. His objective was the town of Uzita, which was strongly garrisoned by Scipio's men, and the wide plain in which it was situated. East of the town lay a series of low hills, and Caesar occupied the first three of these, digging an entrenchment to protect his position from attack from the west. Scipio and Labienus, on seeing what was going on, drew up their cavalry and their infantry in battle line and advanced toward the camp. Caesar also formed line of battle, but before the two met, a cavalry engagement developed, in which Scipio's cavalry was driven from the field. The Pompeian infantry panicked and fled back to their camp.

Subsequently Caesar occupied the line of hills and then decided to attack Uzita itself. To protect his forces as they advanced across the plain toward the town, he had two parallel entrenchments dug from his camp westward, a distance of about 2 miles. Less than 100 yards from the town he built a camp between the ends of the two trenches, and put five legions there to hold it.

While this work was going on, Caesar sent out two squadrons of ships, under Lucius Cispius and Quintus Aquila, to watch for additional reinforcements expected to arrive from Sicily. Publius Attius Varus, the Pompeian naval commander, however, had also learned that the transports were approaching and put to sea with fifty-five galleys to intercept them. He went first to Leptis, where he burned five of Caesar's transports, which were anchored there, and captured two galleys.

When Caesar learned of this he was furious. He left his army and with a small escort galloped rapidly to Leptis. There he ordered the sailors to man the few remaining galleys and then himself led the squadron out to sea. He sailed north until he encountered Aquila's squadron. Taking command of those ships, Caesar then set off after Varus.

Despite his advantage in numbers, Varus was so surprised by Caesar's precipitate action that he turned his fleet and fled to the safety of Hadrumetum. Caesar caught up with the last vessels of the Pompeian fleet and captured two galleys and some transports. After burning the transports he sailed back to Leptis. By vigor and good luck, Caesar had turned a minor setback into a victory, and had probably prevented a disaster.

The transports from Sicily arrived soon thereafter, bringing two more legions, which raised the strength of Caesar's army to nine legions, probably about 30,000 men in all. Almost at once he formed them all in battle line facing Scipio's army near Uzita. But neither side attacked; Caesar waited because he was so greatly outnumbered—the Pompeians because they so greatly feared Caesar. Caesar's foragers later defeated a force sent by Labienus to ambush them on one of their forays but, except for a few skirmishes, for several weeks there was no other action between the two armies.

When the grain supply again became a problem Caesar decided to move. This time he marched farther south and encamped near Aggar. Scipio and Juba—who had rejoined the Pompeians—followed him. They made their camps about 6 miles to the west, near the town of Tegea.

Scipio sent out two legions to forage near a town called Zeta (Beni Hassan), about 10 miles north of his camp and 14 miles from that of Caesar. Caesar thought this might provide an opportunity to entice the Pompeians into battle under circumstances favorable to him. He marched for Zeta with his whole army, leaving only a small garrison in his camp. He passed the main enemy camp and moved into Zeta with no opposition. Scipio's two foraging legions were still farther on.

When Caesar saw reinforcements hurrying up from Scipio's camp he left a garrison in Zeta and marched back toward his own camp. Suddenly Labienus and Afranius, with cavalry and lightly armed troops, attacked the rear of his line. Caesar drove them off, only to have them return to the attack from all sides as soon as he had again formed in marching order. By repeating these tactics the Pompeians delayed him, and it took Caesar's army several hours to reach their camp.

The operation had not turned out as Caesar had hoped. But the Pompeian-Numidian combination of cavalry and lightly armed troops impressed Caesar. Up to this time he had not been able to counter these tactics; now he decided to train some of his men to operate in similar fashion. He devoted the next few weeks to this. When, on March 23, he attempted to take the town of Sarsura, where Scipio had stored grain, Caesar's newly trained cavalry and lightly armed infantry drove off Labienus with his own tactics.

More reinforcements arrived at about this time, bringing the number of men available to Caesar to about 35,000 legionaries, 4,000 cavalry, and 2,000 archers and slingers. With this strength he believed he could risk battle with the Pompeians. He decided to strike at one of Scipio's main bases, Thapsus. The praetor Caius Vergilius was in command at Thapsus with a large garrison.

Battle of Thapsus

Thapsus was on the coast about 16 miles north of Aggar. A few miles inland a long, shallow lake (the Marsh of Moknine) prevented a direct approach to the town. Access was thus re-

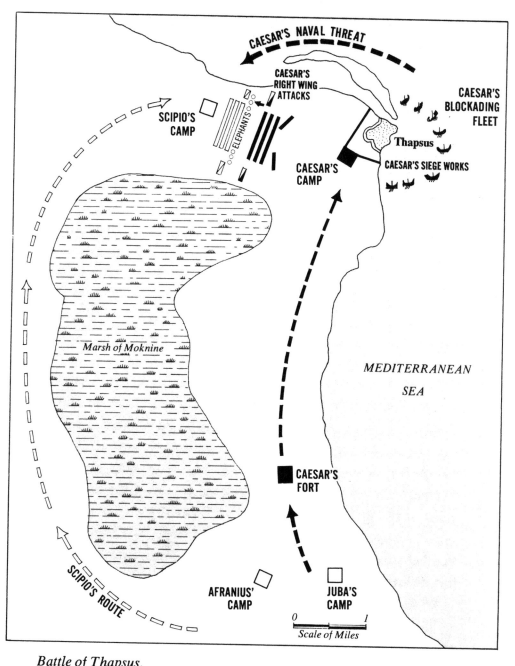

Battle of Thapsus.

stricted to a narrow corridor that could be entered from either south or west. In this area, varying from 1½ to 3 miles in width, the Numidian cavalry would be severely hampered in their encirclement tactics.

During the night of April 4, Caesar marched from the south along the coast. He left three cohorts at the entrance to the approach corridor about 8 miles from Thapsus, with orders to build a fort there. With the rest of his men he advanced to Thapsus. There he encamped close by the walls and began to build a ring of siege works around the landward side of the town. Scipio followed as far as the fort, where he left Juba and Afranius in two camps. He then marched around the lake and entered the other approach corridor, encamping about 2 miles from Caesar, to the west of the town.

Caesar's fleet was blockading the sea approach to Thapsus. He ordered the fleet to be prepared, at a given signal, to send a squadron close inshore at the rear of Scipio's army. Leaving two legions in his camp, Caesar marched out toward Scipio, who had drawn up his army outside his camp, with thirty-two elephants on each wing of his legions. Caesar drew up his legions in the usual three lines, with his cavalry and new lightly armed troops on the wings. As he had done at Pharsalus, he put five cohorts, with archers and slingers, in a fourth, oblique line behind each wing, this time to deal with the elephants.

While Caesar was addressing his troops before battle in the customary fashion, so much confusion was noticed in the enemy's lines that Caesar's men became excited. Without orders, his right wing charged, followed by all the other troops.

162

The arrows and stones of Caesar's archers and slingers so upset the elephants that they turned and trampled their own men. Then, as Caesar's fleet approached the shore behind them, the Numidian cavalry panicked. Soon the entire Pompeian army was fleeing in confusion.

Caesar left part of his army to pursue the defeated foe, and hurried south with the rest toward the camps of Juba and Afranius. But word had already reached them of Scipio's defeat and the leaders had fled, leaving their troops in complete confusion. Caesar was unable to restrain his men from massacring the Pompeian troops and then plundering the camps. It was reported that the Pompeians lost 10,000 men in the battle and Caesar scarcely 50.

This was the beginning of the end for the Pompeians in Africa. Thapsus and Thysdra, the only sizable strongholds remaining, soon surrendered to Caesar. He marched to seize Uzita and Hadrumetum, and then on to Utica. Most of the leaders of the Pompeians were eliminated. Juba and Petreius fought a duel in which one killed the other and then himself. Afranius was surrendered to Caesar, who put him to death. Cato committed suicide. Scipio, trying to flee by ship, was run down and drowned.

Belated Triumph in Rome

Caesar incorporated the kingdom of Juba in the Roman province of Africa and then returned to Rome in late July.

On his arrival Caesar received honors such as had never before been known in Rome. The Senate had prolonged his dictatorship to ten years. A celebration of forty days was decreed for the victory of Thapsus. Among other honors granted by the Senate were his appointment as Prefect of Morals; his triumphal chariot was set opposite Jupiter's on the Capitoline Hill; a statue of him as a demigod was erected on a monument representing the world.

At last Caesar had his triumph for his victory over the Gauls —and following it Vercingetorix was put to death. There were three more triumphs: for his victories over the Egyptians, Pharnaces, and Juba. (Triumphs were restricted to victories over foreign enemies.) There followed a great feast for which 22,000 tables were spread. Then came many days of spectacles of every kind—lion hunts, individual and group gladiatorial contests, a naval battle on an artificial lake constructed on the Campus Martius, and finally a great battle in which more than 1,000 prisoners fought to the death. From the immense wealth Caesar brought to Rome, each Roman received 300 sesterces,* 10 pecks of grain, and 10 pounds of oil.

Caesar stayed in Rome long enough to enact a number of laws and reforms, of which the most significant from the viewpoint of history was his reform of the calendar. Having become acquainted with the Egyptian calendar, which for centuries had

---

* The exact value of the sesterce is not known. It was one quarter of the basic Roman coin, the denarius, which was probably not worth more than fifty cents (1968). Thus 300 sesterces may have been worth about $35.00.

been based on the movements of the sun, he adopted it for Rome in place of the lunar calendar, which by that time had gotten far out of line with the seasons. With the assistance of the Egyptian astronomer Sosigenes, Caesar set the length of the year at 365¼ days—three years of 365 days followed by one of 366. To alternate months he assigned 31 and 30 days, with the exception of February, which received 29, with 30 every fourth year. Except for some rearrangement of numbers of days for some months made by Augustus*, and a slight modification by Pope Gregory XIII in the sixteenth century, the calendar remains the same today.

Cleopatra with a large retinue arrived in Rome during Caesar's visit, bringing with her Caesar's baby son, Caesarion. Caesar installed her in his house in the suburbs of Rome and even placed a statue of her in the temple of Venus Genetrix, beside that of the goddess herself.

To Spain

Caesar had appointed Quintus Cassius as governor of Spain, but he had proved to be incompetent and corrupt. Following the Battle of Pharsalus, two of Cassius' legions had revolted.

* The month of July, named after Julius Caesar, had 31 days. The next month was renamed August, in honor of his successor, Augustus, who also wanted 31 days in his month. So, one day was taken from February, and the sequence of months alternating between 30 and 31 days was changed after August.

165

Only with great difficulty was the revolt put down. Cassius was finally replaced by Trebonius. The legions mutinied while Caesar was in Africa, and they expelled Trebonius.

Pompey's son Gnaeus, hearing of the revolt, went to Spain. He was greeted by his father's old legions and was elected commander in chief of the rebellious army. Labienus, Sextus, Varus, and other fugitives from Africa soon joined Gnaeus' force, and many of the local inhabitants flocked to his support. Caesar's legates in Spain, Quintus Pedius and Fabius Maximus, sent an urgent plea for help. Thus, early in November, 46 B.C., Caesar was on his way to Spain, bringing reinforcements with him.

So rapidly did Caesar travel that he arrived near Corduba, a distance of 1,500 miles, in twenty-seven days, and everyone was surprised to see him. He had at his disposal there eight legions and 8,000 cavalry. Gnaeus had thirteen legions, but only four of these were much good. When Caesar reached Obulco (Porcuna), 35 miles east of Corduba, he found that Sextus was holding Corduba with two legions, and Gnaeus was besieging Ulia. Caesar at once sent six cohorts and some horsemen to Ulia, while he marched to attack Corduba.

When he reached Corduba, Caesar sent a picked force of cavalry and infantry close to the city, enticing Sextus to attack. Caesar's counterattack drove Sextus back into the city, and he sent to Gnaeus for help. By the time Gnaeus arrived, Caesar had built three camps and invested the city. A number of skirmishes took place, but Gnaeus refused to accept battle.

Caesar's supplies were running low. He decided to leave

166

Corduba and moved to Ategua (Teba), which the Pompeians had strongly garrisoned and where they had a large supply of grain. Gnaeus did not follow until he learned that Caesar had laid siege to the town and was building lines of contravallation. Then Gnaeus approached, and a series of small actions followed, marked by brutality on both sides. Within the city the inhabitants and the garrison quarreled, for the noncombatants wished to surrender. Finally, after an attempt by the garrison to cut its way out through Caesar's lines was repulsed, the garrison surrendered. Caesar occupied the town on February 19.

Then Gnaeus withdrew, probably to the south, followed by Caesar. Gnaeus moved from place to place until March 16, when he reached the fortress of Munda, probably between the Salsum (Guadajoz) River and the Singulis (Peinado) River, not far from modern Osuna. (The exact location of Munda is not known today.) Munda was built on a hill beside a plain through which ran a rivulet. Caesar encamped in the plain, not far from Gnaeus, whose camp was on the high ground.

Battle of Munda

Caesar was preparing to move to another location on the morning after his arrival, when he learned that Gnaeus' army was deployed for battle on the hillside near its camp. The Pompeians were in the usual formation, the thirteen legions in the center flanked by cavalry and auxiliaries, with more auxiliaries in the rear. He had about 45,000 men.

Caesar at once formed up his army, with the eight legions also in the center of his line. The 10th was on the right and the 3rd and 5th were on the left. Included with his cavalry was a corps of Africans led by King Bogud of Mauretania (Morocco). Caesar's men were impatient for a fight, and he was confident that their enthusiasm and experience would overcome the disadvantages of their smaller numbers—some 35,000—and of fighting uphill.

The several accounts of the battle are confused and sometimes conflicting, but the main outline is clear. From the first volley of heavy javelins from both sides, as the front lines approached each other, the fighting was intense. Men on both sides wielded their swords fiercely. As those in the front lines tired or fell wounded the lines in back moved up. Caesar was in the thick of the fight, urging his men on and often participating himself. The outcome was in doubt until late in the day.

Apparently Bogud and his cavalry, after several hours of fierce fighting, rode around to threaten the enemy camp. Labienus, seeing the danger, ordered five cohorts to that area. At the same time the 10th Legion renewed its efforts against Gnaeus' left wing. The Pompeian legionaries, seeing Labienus' men move back, thought they were retreating, and faltered. It was enough. Led by the 10th Legion, Caesar's men pushed through and their opponents fled from the field.

Pursued to their camp, the Pompeians stood their ground until they were slaughtered. Some 30,000 were said to have perished, although this figure is probably exaggerated. Many took refuge in the fortress at Munda, where Caesar at once besieged

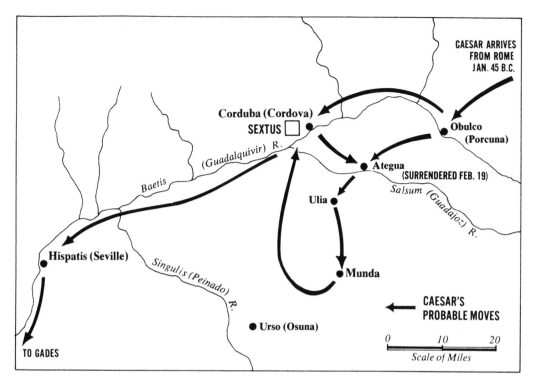

Battle of Munda.

them. He reported only 1,000 of his men killed and 500 wounded, probably also inaccurate since he must have lost many more men in the desperate struggle.

The Battle of Munda was apparently the fiercest of the whole civil war. Victory for Caesar was not certain for hours. As he left the field, says Plutarch, Caesar remarked "that he had often striven for victory, but now first for his life." Had he lost he would surely have perished, as did Labienus and Attius Varus. Gnaeus escaped but was finally captured as he tried to get away by sea from Spain. He was beheaded.

Leaving Fabius Maximus to maintain the siege at Munda, Caesar again marched to Corduba. Sextus Pompeius had fled

169

from the city, leaving his two legions quarreling with each other. One wished to surrender, the other to resist. When Caesar arrived, the single opposing legion was easily overcome.

Caesar then went on to Hispalis (Seville), Asta (Mesa de Asta), and Gades, in each place encountering and overwhelming supporters of Pompey. During the spring and summer he continued the pacification, until he felt sure that Spain was sufficiently subdued. In late summer he sailed for Italy, accompanied by his eighteen-year-old grand nephew Octavius, grandson of his sister Julia. By mid-September of 45 B.C. Caesar was back in Rome.

CHAPTER 11

Foundation of Empire

Honors and Reforms

The civil war was at last over, and there was no one strong enough to challenge Caesar's exercise of supreme power in Rome. He had a great army and untold wealth. Nothing was beyond his reach that could be taken by force or bought by money.

The people of Rome heaped more and more honors upon Caesar, and he accepted them all. His victories in Spain were celebrated with fifty days of thanksgiving and a triumph, even though they had been won over Romans and not over foreign kings. He was given the title of Imperator for life, and this was to be passed along to his heirs. He was elected consul for ten years and given supreme control of financial matters in Rome. He was even raised to the rank of a god. A statue of him, inscribed "To the Invincible God," was ordered set up in the temple of the deified Romulus, legendary founder of Rome, and another was put beside the former kings on the Capitoline Hill. Caesar's statue, carved in ivory, was to be carried with those of the gods at public games.

171

All of this would have taxed the modesty of the most humble of men, but Caesar was neither humble nor modest. He increased his own power at the expense of the Senate, clearly intending to move far from the old Republican constitution.

Caesar's admirers say that he was attempting to bring stability to Rome by changing the governmental weaknesses that had led to nearly half a century of internal strife. His detractors insist that he was satisfying his lust for power and authority. Both are probably partly right.

In the next few months Caesar made many changes. He pardoned most of his opponents in a general amnesty. Perhaps foolishly, he put many in positions where later they could, and did, do him harm. He increased the number of praetors and quaestors and raised the Senate membership, adding to it his friends of all classes, including Gauls. Through his position as supervisor of morals, he threatened to expel from the Senate anyone who displeased him. He could issue edicts independently of the Senate, and new magistrates entering office were forced to swear obedience to these edicts.

Caesar instituted a number of measures which made the government more liberal and more efficient, and which assured a sound economy. Where these changes might have led is impossible to tell, for there is no record of what he had in mind for the future. His reforms won him great popularity with the people and made more enemies among the conservatives.

Although Caesar's reforms were not completed, he felt that he should leave Rome to deal with threats to the eastern borders of the provinces. A powerful Thracian kingdom had been building up on the Danube, threatening the Greek cities on the Black Sea. On the borders of Syria and Asia Minor the Parthians were again a menace, and the defeat they had inflicted on Crassus at Carrhae had not been avenged. So Caesar planned to deal first with the Thracians and then to march against Parthia, extending the boundaries of the empire. In preparation for these campaigns he ordered the assembly in Illyricum of sixteen legions and 10,000 cavalry. He planned to join in mid-March of 44 B.C.

Master of the World

At the beginning of 44 B.C. the Senate heaped still more honors on Caesar. He accepted these while seated in the temple of Benus Genetrix. His failure to rise was held by some to be a sign of contempt for the Senate, and many senators were deeply offended. However, when he learned of this reaction, Caesar apologized, saying that he had been ill.

Caesar apparently was fully satisfied with what he had won, but his friends kept trying to push him to accept more honors and power. Whether he coveted the kingship has been the subject of much discussion. On February 15, having just accepted the dictatorship for life, he was offered a crown by Antony, during a great public celebration.

Caesar refused it, reportedly with the words, "Jupiter alone is King of the Romans." The people applauded loudly. But many believe he would have accepted the crown if the people had asked him to. Whether or not he wished to be king, Caesar's position of power was entirely unprecedented in the Roman Republic, which had traditionally opposed the exercise of supreme political or military power by any one man, save in time of grave crisis.

The Ides of March

There were many Romans who feared or hated Caesar, either because of his power, or because they disliked his reforms, or who feared his measures would mean financial ruin for themselves and perhaps for Rome. These men believed that there should be a return to the old Roman Republic. Gradually a conspiracy to kill Caesar was developed among these people.

There is little evidence of how the conspiracy started. More than sixty men were involved in it, and many of them had been close friends or supporters of Caesar. Gaius Cassius—who Caesar realized was no friend—seems to have been the ringleader. Marcus Brutus, a young man who had become one of Caesar's favorite assistants, was also among the active ones. Both had fought for Pompey at Pharsalus, and been pardoned by Caesar after the battle.

The date for Caesar's departure on the Eastern campaign was set for March 18. It had been prophesied that only a king would conquer Parthia. The likelihood was great that a motion to make Caesar king before he left would be made in the Senate, and the conspirators did not wish to risk voting against it. So they decided the deed must be done on what the Roman calendar called the Ides of March—March 15.

Various bad omens caused Caesar to tell Antony on the morning of March 15 that he would not go to the Senate and that it should be dismissed. The conspirators grew nervous when Caesar did not appear and finally sent Decimus Brutus, whom Caesar trusted, to urge him to come. Brutus persuaded him that he should go himself and tell the Senate that he wished to postpone the meeting.

Before entering the Senate House, Caesar once more consulted the will of the gods in accordance with Roman custom. Again the signs were inauspicious. But Caesar laughed at them and proceeded. When he was seated in his gilded chair the assassins clustered around him, and then suddenly fell upon him with their daggers. Bravely the astonished dictator attempted to defend himself. But, according to legend, when he saw Brutus* wielding a knife against him, he said, "*Et tu Brute*—'And thou, Brutus!'," ceased his struggles, and drew his toga over his eyes. At the foot of Pompey's statue he fell dead, blood flowing from twenty-three wounds.

---

* It is generally assumed that it was the sight of Marcus Brutus which was so shocking to Caesar. Some authorities, however, believe that it may have been Decimus Brutus.

175

Epilogue

After the assassination of Caesar, the senators fled from the building. The conspirators, who had no plan for restoring order once the deed was done, also ran from the hall and addressed the crowds of people outside, calling on them "to restore the government of their fathers." All was confusion.

There were two men in position to pick up the reins—Mark Antony, who was consul with Caesar for the year 44 B.C., and Marcus Aemilius Lepidus, who was Magister Equitum, the principal military officer under the consuls. Lepidus favored bringing up troops to attack the assassins in their hiding places, but Antony dissuaded him. He went at once to Caesar's wife and secured from her the money and papers of the fallen dictator. Calling the Senate together he calmed down those who demanded prompt revenge and pointed out the folly of making any immediate changes. Persuaded by Antony, the Senate passed a decree stating, "There shall be no prosecutions for the murder of Caesar, but all his acts and decrees are confirmed, because his policy is deemed advantageous to the commonwealth."

176

Caesar's will, which was read to the assembled populace, adopted his grand-nephew Octavius as his son and personal heir. He left his gardens to the Roman people for use as a public park, and to every citizen of Rome he left 300 sesterces. At Caesar's funeral Antony's eloquent oration so aroused the anger of the Roman people that they set fire to the building where he had been murdered, burned the houses of the assassins, and caused them to flee from the city. Antony also won for himself great popularity with the Roman public.

Octavius was eighteen years old when Caesar died. He was at Apollonia when he learned of the assassination, and he started at once for Rome. On the way he heard that he had been adopted by the will of the fallen dictator, and he determined to claim the political as well as the personal inheritance.

But when Octavius reached Rome he found that Antony had no intention of yielding any of the power that he had begun to consolidate for himself. He refused to turn over Octavius' inheritance or even to pay the promised 300 sesterces to each Roman citizen. So Octavius, who changed his name to Gaius Julius Caesar Octavianus, took the responsibility for it, selling his family property to pay the populace from his own pocket.

In the following years Rome returned to the conditions of turmoil that Caesar thought he had ended by his victories and his reforms. Antony had persuaded the Senate to pardon the conspirators and several of these became involved in the confused struggle for power. But by the close of 43 B.C. two men had achieved preeminence: Octavius and Antony. Neither had shown great military talent, but both were adroit politicans, and each could claim to be the heir of Caesar: Antony the political heir, and Octavius the personal and family heir.

Although it seemed inevitable that these two men were headed for a final struggle for power, young Octavius was not yet ready to confront Antony. Instead he made overtures to Antony, and met with Antony and Lepidus at Bononia (Bologna) in November, 43 B.C. They agreed to make themselves *tresviri rei publicae constituendae*, commissioners with unlimited power to reorganize the state. The law establishing the Second Triumvirate was passed on November 27, 43 B.C.

The reign of the Triumvirate began with a wholesale massacre in which 300 senators, including Cicero, and 2,000 other leading Romans were killed. Thousands more fled from Italy. The purpose of this horror was not only to remove political opponents from the scene but to acquire lands and money by confiscation, to help pay the Triumvirs' troops.

Marcus Brutus and Cassius meanwhile had by the end of 43 B.C. secured control of many of the eastern provinces of Rome, and had acquired a strong fleet. Early in the following year, Antony and Octavius marched to Macedonia to attack them. After two confused and uninspired battles, Antony defeated the two conspirators at Philippi. Both Brutus and Cassius committed suicide.

Following the final defeat of the assassins, it was arranged that Antony should stay in the East and collect money for the Triumvirate armies, and Octavius should return to Italy and find land for 110,000 veterans. Lepidus had already taken Africa as his area of responsibility.

In following months Octavius confiscated land in eighteen

prosperous areas of Italy and divided it among the men. But Antony soon found that Brutus and Cassius had done such a thorough job of plundering the East that only Egypt offered any hope of providing the wealth he needed. He met Cleopatra at Tarsus and he seems to have acquired Egypt peacefully by the simple means of making Cleopatra his wife.

Octavius, in the meantime, had become much disliked in Italy because of his confiscation of land. Antony's wife Fulvia —who apparently did not yet know about Cleopatra—and his brother Lucius Antonius tried to take advantage of this antagonism to promote Antony over Octavius. Fighting broke out, and Octavius finally defeated Lucius at the Battle of Perusia in 40 B.C.

Meanwhile the Parthians had invaded Asia Minor, and it became necessary for Antony to go to its defense. To do so he needed reinforcements from Italy, but Octavius was understandably reluctant to permit Antony to recruit there. Finally the two met at Brundisium, together with Lepidus, and with Sextus Pompeius—surviving son of Pompey—who was in control of Sicily. From this meeting came an agreement to continue a joint rule in Italy, to assign the western provinces to Octavius, Africa to Lepidus, the East to Antony, and Sardinia, Sicily, and Greece to Sextus Pompey. Antony—whose wife Fulvia had recently died—then married the sister of Octavius, Octavia, to seal the alliance.

Despite this agreement Octavius renewed the fight with Sextus. After a series of battles Sextus was defeated in 36 B.C. and fled to Asia Minor where he was finally killed. Lepidus tried to claim Sicily, but his troops deserted him for Octavius,

179

ending his political power. Octavius, meanwhile, had begun to regain his popularity in Italy. The Senate awarded him the rights of a tribune.

Antony, since embarking on the compaigns in Asia, had grown closer to Cleopatra and farther from Octavia. Yielding to Cleopatra's demands, he made over some of his lands in Italy to her children. After 35 B.C. he refused even to see Octavia, and in 32 B.C., Octavia, divorced him.

The triumvirate law expired in 32 B.C., and Octavius, who was elected consul for 31 B.C., declared war on Cleopatra. He carefully avoided a declaration against Antony. Antony and Cleopatra went to Greece and based their army and powerful fleet at Actium. There in September, 31 B.C., occurred a naval engagement in which most of Antony's and Cleopatra's fleet was destroyed, although they themselves escaped to Egypt. Most of their army surrendered to Octavius. The rest was dispersed.

Antony and Cleopatra—followed by Octavius to Egypt— found themselves with virtually no army. The approach of Octavius drove Antony to commit suicide. When Octavius showed that he was unimpressed by her beauty, Cleopatra also took her own life.

So ended the long years of civil wars. Octavius made Egypt a province and carried off the royal treasure in triumph to Rome. Now he alone remained, sole ruler of the Roman Empire. After a delay of fourteen years, the probable plans and intentions of Julius Caesar became reality with his grand-nephew who inherited his power. Octavius was henceforth known as Augustus Caesar.

Chronology

	October	Caesar lands at Alexandria, Egypt.
47,	June	Caesar leaves Egypt.
	August 2	Battle of Zela.
		Caesar's second dictatorship.
	December 25	Caesar sails for Africa.
46,	January	Battle of Ruspina.
	April	Battle of Thapsus.
	July 25	Caesar returns to Rome; dictatorship extended to ten years.
	November	Caesar leaves for Spain.
45,	March 17	Battle of Munda.
	September	Caesar returns to Rome.
44,	March 15	Caesar assassinated.
43		Second Triumvirate.
42		Battles of Philippi.
31		Battle of Actium.
30		Suicides of Antony and Cleopatra; Octavius supreme in Rome as Augustus Caesar.

Appendix

Principles of Military Leadership and Military Theory

Since different people have different ideas about leadership and about how it is defined and recognized, a few paragraphs are necessary to explain how the word "leadership" is applied in this book to the military career of one of the outstanding men of history.

Military Leadership

In its simplest terms, *leadership* means the ability of a person to influence and direct other people to work cooperatively together toward a goal or objective, because that individual commands their obedience, confidence, and respect. But these words are really meaningful only if we can relate them to observable standards of performance. One set of standards to show the qualities of a military leader is the following:

Professional military skill or competence. This includes a knowledge and understanding of past military events (or military history), an understanding of theoretical principles of warfare, and a combination of judgment and energy in applying this knowledge and theory to a variety of different situations.

Understanding of the human tools of the leader. This simply means that a leader must know the capabilities and limitations of his men.

Insistence upon high standards of training and discipline. In this way the leader, knowing his men, is able to make the most of their capabilities and to eliminate or reduce their weaknesses and limitations.

Inspirational ability. The leader must be able to project his personality to his men, so that they recognize the quality of his leadership and respond to it with confidence.

Personal courage. The leader must be able to set an example for his men. But in addition to willingness to face the dangers and risks of battle, he must have moral courage off the battlefield to make difficult decisions which lesser men might try to avoid.

Perseverance and determination in adversity. Some men can perform well when everything seems to be going their way. One important measure of human greatness is a person's ability to keep on striving for success, even when his best plans and actions seem to be resulting in failure.

The ability, in peace and war, to understand the relationship between military strategy and national policy. This is as true of a king-general, like Alexander the Great, or a civilian director of war, like Winston Churchill, as it is of the general who is controlled by civilian authority, like George Washington.

These are the seven standards, or yardsticks, of leadership which provide a basis for selecting the great captains. All of these standards are simple, and easy to understand, although their relationship together is so difficult that only a handful of men have been able to measure up close to the maximum of all of these standards.

The reader who is not intimately acquainted with military theory may find some problems with the first of the above standards, in recognizing the ability of a leader to apply military theory and principles to different situations. All that we really need to know, however, to understand the professional military qualities of military leadership which made the great captains great, is the nature of the principles of war and the relationship between strategy and tactics.

Military Theory

Over the past century, military theorists have formulated lists of *Principles of War* which are believed to include all of the fundamental elements of success in waging war. There are some differences among the lists prepared by different theorists, but since they are all based upon review and analysis of historical examples, these various lists are generally consistent with each other. There are differences of opinion as to the applicability of these principles to warfare in the future, but there is no doubt that they provide a useful measurement for past conflicts, since they are derived from, and based upon, the experience of the past.

In this series we use the following list of nine principles of war:

Objective. Every military operation should be directed to accomplish a decisive, realistic objective. The ultimate objective of any conflict is to destroy the enemy's capability and desire to continue the conflict. Intermediate objectives should contribute directly to attaining this ultimate objective. Objectives should be selected after due consideration of the characteristics of the area of conflict, and the resources and military forces which both sides can employ in the conflict.

Offensive. Only offensive action can achieve decisive results, since only by attacking or advancing can a military leader accomplish his objective by forcing his will on the enemy. Sometimes circumstances are such that a commander must take defensive action because the enemy is stronger, or in a more favorable position. But a leader on the defensive should always be seeking to find an opportunity where he can seize the initiative and press toward the achievement of his objective by offensive action. Other principles of war can help him in this search.

Simplicity. A commander must plan his operations and organize his forces so that they are as simple and uncomplicated as possible. When hundreds or thousands of men must work together to accomplish a plan, even the most simple plan may fail. The possibility for confusion and failure is even greater when men and commanders are frightened and excited in the course of a battle.

Control. (This is sometimes called "Unity of Command" or "Cooperation.") There must be one controlling authority to assure the decisive employment of all men and forces toward the achievement of an objective. This controlling authority achieves unity of effort by coordinating the actions of all forces available to him and assures cooperation between all of the individual people or forces engaged in the conflict.

187

Mass. (This is sometimes called "Concentration.") The maximum available combat power should be applied at the point and at the time which will best assure a decisive success. By seizing the initiative and concentrating forces rapidly and efficiently, a smaller force can often apply greater combat power at the decisive point than a larger enemy force. Mass is not dependent upon numbers alone but results from a combination of manpower, firepower, and fighting capability. Superior weapons, tactics, and morale can contribute to the effectiveness of mass.

Economy of Forces. (This is sometimes called "Economy of Effort.") A commander should employ only the absolute minimum of forces or resources at points which are not decisive. This will permit him to accomplish the principles of the objective and of mass at decisive times and places. Defensive action, or deception, at the less important points will help a commander achieve economy of forces.

Maneuver. Maneuver is the positioning, or the moving, of forces in such a way as to place the enemy at a relative disadvantage. By maneuver a commander can apply the principles of mass and the offensive at a decisive point where the enemy is not adequately prepared or positioned to meet an attack.

Surprise. This is accomplished by striking an enemy at a time, or in a place, or in a manner, that he does not expect. Surprise is particularly important for the commander of a force which does not otherwise have combat superiority to the enemy. Surprise can be achieved by speed, secrecy, deception, variations in fighting methods, and by moving through regions which the enemy does not think are passable for military forces.

Security. This means that a commander must take those measures which will prevent the enemy from surprising him, or from interfering with his operations. With adequate security, a commander can then apply the other principles of war, and employ his own forces in the most effective manner possible.

These principles of war are obviously very general in their nature; they apply to large forces and to small, and to extensive campaigns as well as to brief engagements. Military men usually say that they are applicable to both tactical and strategic operations. This means that the nonmilitary reader should have a clear understanding of the difference between strategy and tactics.

Many, many thousands of words have been written to describe strategy and tactics, and to explain the difference between the two terms. But really the distinction is not difficult.

Military strategy is the art of employing all of the resources available to a military commander for the purpose of achieving a successful outcome in a conflict against hostile armed forces.

Military tactics is the technique of assembling, positioning, and moving some specific portion of the forces available to a commander in order to contribute to the accomplishment of the goals or objectives of strategy.

In other words, strategy concerns the employment and disposition of all means of forces within a commander's power in order to achieve the desired result of a war or campaign. Tactics concerns the specific battlefield methods of employment of these means or forces.

189

Index